THE CLASSIC STEP-BY-STEP SERIES

MARY FORD

CAKE & BISCUIT RECIPES

With easy to follow instructions

INTRODUCTION

There is nothing more satisfying than spending a couple of hours in one's kitchen baking - perhaps a few simple flapjacks, or maybe a wickedly gooey chocolate cake. Especially when the results are greeted with glowing praise and admiration from one's family and friends.

Over the many years I have spent working in baking, I have come across so many delicious recipes for cakes, biscuits and traybakes that I have decided to put them all together in one book. The recipes are presented in my highly successful "Classic Step-by-Step" formula, with clear captions and colour photographs to guide you through every stage. In addition, most recipes incorporate "Mary's Tips", to give you a bit of extra help or an interesting variation.

The ingredients used are all readily available in supermarkets and the recipes do not require anything more than the most basic baking equipment found in most domestic kitchens. The recipes selected cater for all tastes and levels of experience in home baking. Indeed, I have included many ideas that are suitable for children to make, watched over by an adult. I hope that it becomes apparent when using the book that making appetising cakes and biscuits can be fast and fun, and is more a question of assembling the correct ingredients and following the instructions than of being an experienced baker.

I very much hope that you enjoy using these recipes as much as I have and that they provide many happy hours of baking and eating.

AUTHOR

Mary Ford has been teaching the art of cake-making and decorating for three decades. Working with her husband, Michael, she has produced over 20 step-by-step books demonstrating the various skills and techniques of the craft, which have sold over 800,000 copies worldwide. Her books have gained an international reputation for expertise and imagination, combined with common sense and practical teaching ability. Her unique step-by-step approach with the emphasis on self-explanatory colour illustrations is ideally suited for both beginners and enthusiasts. Having run her own bakery business for many years, she remains an enthusiastic home-baker and "Cake and Biscuit Recipes" brings her many years of experience to everyone who enjoys baking at home.

CONTENTS

GETTING STARTED

THE RECIPES

Take care when adjusting the quantities of the recipe; although doubling the ingredients for twice the quantity may work for some cakes, I would strongly recommend you stick to the quantities given, as these have produced proven cakes.

INGREDIENTS

Assemble all the ingredients and leave them to stand at room temperature for at least an hour before starting to cook to avoid curdling the mixture. I find size 3 eggs the most successful for baking.

TINS

Always grease the tin and if possible line the base. Never bake in a brand new tin: bake off the shininess in a hot oven and allow to cool before use. Do not rush to get the cake out of the tin once cooked - many cakes are liable to crack if handled too early. The richer the cake, the longer it should be left to cool.

OVENS

In general, fan-assisted ovens cook more quickly than conventional and electric is faster than gas. There is no substitute to knowing your own oven, but I suggest you buy a thermometer (I recommend Brannan), to ensure pinpoint accuracy.

Never forget the skewer - only if it comes out clean is the mixture cooked. Try to resist opening the oven door during cooking. Set the timer and wait for the buzzer.

STORAGE

Store in an airtight container in a cool, dry place. Cakes also freeze successfully for up to six months.

MAKING BUTTERCREAM

The rule for buttercream is: the longer you beat the lighter it becomes, both in texture and colour.

INGREDIENTS

Metric		Imperial
170g	Unsalted butter	6oz
341g	Sieved icing sugar	12oz
45ml	Warm water	3tbsp

All ingredients should be warmed to 65/70°.

Soften butter and beat until light.

Gradually add the icing sugar, beating well after each addition.

Beat in the water.

Colour and flavour with chocolate, cocoa etc. if required.

MARY FORD

CAKE RECIPES

SIMPLE SPONGE CAKE

INGREDIENTS

Metric		Imperial
	1½ eggs, size 3	
85g	Caster sugar	3oz
85g	Self raising flour, sifted	3oz
30ml	Hot water	2tbsp

BAKING TIN

20cm (8in) round sponge tin, greased and floured.

BAKING

Preheated oven, 200°C or 400°F or gas mark 6. When the sponge has been baking for 14 minutes, open the oven door slowly, and if the sponge is pale in colour continue baking. When it is golden brown, draw fingers across the top of it, lightly pressing, and if this leaves indentation, continue baking. Repeat test every 2-3 minutes until the top springs back when touched.

STORAGE

Wrap the cooled sponge in waxed paper and store in an airtight tin, eating it within 3 days. Or freeze for up to 6 months and use within 3 days of defrosting.

Mary's Tips

For a chocolate sponge, follow the same recipe but replace 14g (½oz) of flour with 14g (½oz) of cocoa powder

1. Using a pastry brush, grease tin(s) with white fat.

2. Sprinkle sufficient flour into sponge tin to cover base and side.

3. Gently shake and turn tin until all the grease is covered with flour. Then tap out excess flour.

4. Crack open an egg into a small basin before putting into the mixing bowl. Repeat for each egg (to ensure bad doesn't mix with good).

5. Lightly whisk egg.

6. Pour caster sugar into mixing bowl with the beaten egg.

7. *Whisk briskly until thick and creamy.*

8. *Stir-in the hot water.*

9. *Sprinkle sieved flour on to the mixture.*

10. *Gently fold in flour with a spatula.*

11. *Transfer mixture to the prepared tin(s).*

12. *Place tin(s) near top of pre-heated oven (400°F, 200°C or Gas Mark 6).*

13. *At end of recommended baking time, test sponge in accordance with the instructions on page 6.*

14. *After baking, leave to cool for five minutes. Then remove from tin on to greaseproof paper covered in caster sugar.*

15. *Upturn sponge and place on wire tray until cold. (See instructions for storage on page 6.)*

SIMPLE GENOESE CAKE

INGREDIENTS

Metric		Imperial
85g	Butter	3oz
85g	Margarine	3oz
170g	Caster sugar	6oz
	3 eggs, size 3	
170g	Self raising flour, sifted	6oz

For a chocolate genoese, replace 28g (1oz) of flour with 28g (1oz) of cocoa powder.

BAKING TIN

Use either a 25.5cm (10in) round tin, or a 23cm (9in) square sponge tin, or a 25.5cm (10in) hoop tin.

BAKING

Preheated oven, 190°C or 375°F or gas mark 5, for 20 minutes. When the genoese has been baking for 20 minutes, open the oven door slowly, and if it is still pale, continue baking. When the genoese is golden brown, draw fingers across it, lightly pressing, and if this leaves an indentation, continue baking. Repeat test every 2-3 minutes until the top springs back when touched.

Mary's Tips

The French traditional small cakes – madeleines – baked in shell-shaped individual tins, are made with genoese mixture.

STORAGE

Wrap the cooled genoese in waxed paper and store in an airtight tin. Or freeze in the waxed paper for up to 6 months, and use within 3 days of defrosting.

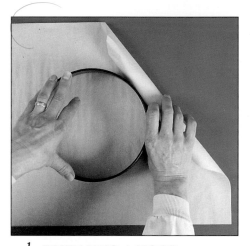

1. **PREPARING A HOOP**
Place a hoop on double sheet of greaseproof paper and roll one corner into side of hoop.

2. Continue rolling paper tightly around the base of the hoop.

3. Tuck in the end of the paper to complete hoop base, then place on baking sheet. Grease inside of hoop and base lightly with white fat.

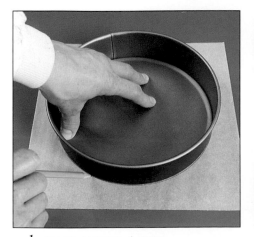

1. **PREPARING A TIN**
Using sponge tin, mark and then cut out a disc of greaseproof paper.

2. Using a pastry brush, grease tin(s) with white fat.

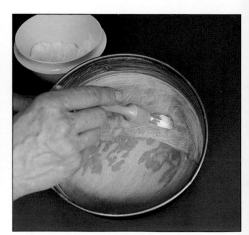

3. Place greaseproof paper disc into bottom of the tin and brush over with white fat.

1. MAKING A GENOESE
Mix then beat the margarine and butter until soft and light.

2. Beat in caster sugar to form a fluffy consistency. Crack open the egg in a separate bowl.

3. Thoroughly beat in a small portion of egg at a time until all egg is used.

4. Pour sieved flour on to mixture.

5. Gently fold flour into mixture. (Don't overmix.)

6. Spoon mixture into prepared hoop(s) or tin(s).

7. Evenly spread mixture with a spatula.

8. Place tin(s) at centre of pre-heated oven (375°F/190°C or Gas Mark 5).

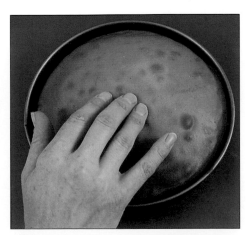

9. At end of recommended baking time, test genoese in accordance with the instructions at the top of page 8. After baking, see Nos. 14/15 on page 7.

MAKING A BASIC FRUIT CAKE

INGREDIENTS
for a 445g (1lb) cake

Metric		Imperial
57g	Plain flour	2oz
57g	Brown sugar	2oz
57g	Butter	2oz
71g	Currants	2½oz
71g	Sultanas	2½oz
28g	Seedless raisins	1oz
28g	Glacé cherries	1oz
42g	Mixed peel	1½oz
21g	Ground almonds	¾oz
2tsp	Brandy or rum	½fl. oz
	1 egg, size 2	
	1 pinch nutmeg	
	1 pinch mixed spice	
	1 pinch salt	
	Zest and juice from	
	¼ lemon.	

SOAKING MIXTURE

Equal quantities of rum, sherry and glycerine, or spirits of your choice: 15ml (1tbsp) per 445g (1lb) of cake, to be brushed on to the cooked cake.

BAKING TIN

Use either a 13cm (5in) round tin, or a 10cm (4in) square tin, approximately 7.5cm (3in) deep, for this basic amount of ingredients. Multiply ingredients for larger cakes, and increase the size of the tin accordingly.

BAKING

Bake at 140°C or 275°F or gas mark 1 for 1¼ hours for a 1lb cake; 1¼ hrs for a 2lb cake; 2½ hrs for a 3lb cake; 3½ hrs for a 4lb cake; 4 hrs for a 5lb cake; 4¼ hrs for a 6lb cake.

At the end of the guide time for baking, test the cake to ensure it is cooked all through. Slide the cake in its tin to the front of the oven. Insert a steel skewer into the centre, slowly remove it, and if it is clean, the cake is ready. If mixture clings to the skewer, lift it out of the cake, slide back the tin and continue testing every 10 minutes.

STORAGE

Wrap the cooled cake in waxed paper – never in clingfilm, tinfoil or a sealed plastic container. Place on a cake board and store in a cool, dry atmosphere which allows odourless air circulation with no direct sunlight.

Although it isn't necessary to freeze this fruit cake, it can be done. But a decorated fruit cake should not be frozen unless the almond paste and icing has been removed first.

Mary's Tips

• Calculate the size of fruit cake you need by using a guide of 8 generous portions from each 445g (1lb) of finished, iced cake.

• A darker fruit cake can be made by substituting 10% of the brown sugar with black treacle.

• If not stored correctly, the cake could become mouldy for various reasons:

– being wrapped while still warm;

– being wrapped after out for too long;

– wrapping it in inferior-quality paper;

– being stored in a variable temperature;

– under-baking;

– too much soaking with alcohol after baking;

– being stored in a damp atmosphere.

• Too hot an oven will produce a cracked crusted top and an uncooked centre. In addition the fruit may be burnt and bitter.

• Too cool an oven will produce uncooked fruit which will dry out quickly and have a very thick crust.

• If the cake has been baked in the correct temperature but the middle sinks, it could be there was too much: liquid in the batter, baking powder, sugar, or fat.

• If the baked cake is crumbly, any of the following could be the cause: curdled batter, overbeaten fat, sugar and eggs, undermixing the flour and fruit, or too little sugar.

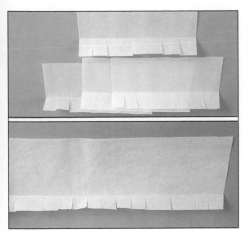

1. Cut greaseproof paper 5cm (2") deeper than cake-tin to cover side(s). (4 pieces for square tin and 1 piece for round tin.)

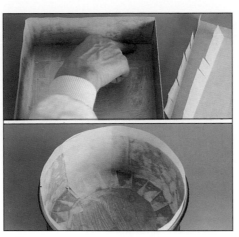

2. Grease tin then cover side(s) and 2.5cm (1") around base with the prepared greaseproof paper. Also ensure paper is 2.5cm (1") above tin height.

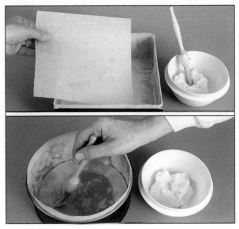

3. Cut greaseproof paper and fit into base of tin, then grease with butter or margarine.

4. Weigh ingredients out onto separate sheets of greaseproof paper, using recipe on page 10, multiplying the ingredients if necessary.

5. Inspect, wash and dry fruit and then chop cherries in half.

6. Grate the lemon and put the zest with the fruit and liquor into a bowl and thoroughly mix.

7. Thoroughly mix and sieve flour, salt and spices on to greaseproof paper several times.

8. Crack open an egg into a small basin before putting into the mixing bowl. Repeat for each egg (to ensure bad doesn't mix with good).

9. Leave all ingredients at room temperature for 12 hours (65°F or 18°C).

10. *Beat butter until light.*

11. *Add and beat in sugar until light.*

12. *Thoroughly beat in a small portion of egg at a time until all egg is used.*

13. *Stir in the ground almonds.*

14. *Add flour and spices to mixture.*

15. *Fold flour and spices lightly into mixture and mix until clear.*

16. *Add fruit and liquor.*

17. *Add lemon juice to mixture.*

18. *Stir mixture thoroughly, but* **DO NOT BEAT**.

19. *Spoon required quantity of mixture into prepared cake tin(s).*

20. *Dip hand in luke warm water and then flatten mixture with the back of wet hand.*

21. *Place cake-tin in centre of pre-heated oven (275°F, 140°C or Gas Mark 1) – with ovenproof bowl containing water beneath.*

22. *At half the baking time, remove water from oven.*

23. *At end of recommended baking time test cake in accordance with instructions on page 10.*

24. *When cake is baked, remove from oven and leave in cool place for 24 hours in the tin.*

25. *Prepare soaking mixture (see page 10).*

26. *Carefully remove greaseproof paper from cake. Upturn cake and brush on soaking mixture (one tablespoon per pound of cake).*

27. *Wrap cake in waxed paper, date it and store cake to mature. (See page 10 for storage instructions.)*

CITRUS CAKE

Serves 8

CHANTILLY GOLD

Mary's Tips

Lemon, orange or lime curd can be used as an alternative.

Double the recipe and divide into three 445g (1lb) loaf tins.

Improves with freezing.

INGREDIENTS

Metric		Imperial
115g	Soft margarine	4oz
100g	Caster sugar	3½oz
	2 eggs, size 2	
30ml	Lemon curd	2tbsp
145g	Self raising flour, sifted	5oz

TOPPING SYRUP

30ml	Granulated sugar dissolved in juice of ½ a lemon.	2tbsp

BAKING TIN

905g (2lb) loaf tin greased and base lined.

BAKING

Preheated oven, 180°C or 360°F or gas mark 4
Middle shelf
50-55 minutes

1. Place all the ingredients into a mixing bowl. Beat until light and fluffy. Do not overbeat.

2. Spoon the mixture into the base lined loaf tin. Place into preheated oven on middle shelf and bake.

3. When baked immediately brush the cake with the topping syrup. Leave cake in tin until cool. Remove from tin and place onto a wire tray until cold.

RHUBARB and DATE CAKE

Serves 12

RAFFLES

1. Sift the flour and baking powder into a bowl. Rub in the margarine to form a fine crumbly texture. Stir in the sugar.

2. Wipe the rhubarb and cut into small cubes. Stir the rhubarb and dates into the mixture.

3. Stir in the beaten egg and milk. Place into the tin, level and bake. After baking leave 10 minutes then turn out onto a wire tray to cool. Dust with icing sugar.

INGREDIENTS

Metric		Imperial
170g	Plain flour	6oz
2.5ml	Baking powder	½tsp
85g	Margarine	3oz
115g	Caster sugar	4oz
225g	Rhubarb	8oz
115g	Stoned dates, chopped	4oz
	1 egg, size 3, beaten	
60ml	Milk	4tbsp

BAKING TIN

16.5cm (6½in) round cake tin greased and lined with greaseproof paper.

BAKING

Preheated oven, 190°C or 370°F or gas mark 5
Middle shelf
1½-2 hours

Mary's Tips

Pale pink forced rhubarb has a mellower flavour than the robust outdoor variety, but both work well with the sweetness of dates.

PEAR and APRICOT CAKE

Serves 8-12

PEAR and APRICOT CAKE

Mary's Tips

Vary the flavour of the filling by using lemon, fruit liqueur or cherry jam.

Sieve icing sugar. However fine, the tiniest lumps can result in roughness. "The longest way round is the shortest way home."

INGREDIENTS

Metric		Imperial
170g	Butter or margarine	6oz
170g	Caster sugar	6oz
	3 eggs, size 2, beaten	
170g	Self raising flour	6oz
57g	Dried pears, chopped	2oz
57g	Dried apricots, chopped	2oz
28g	Glacé cherries, chopped	1oz
28g	Angelica, chopped	1oz

FILLING

57g	Butter	2oz
115g	Icing sugar, sifted	4oz
10ml	Kirsch	2tsp
	1 egg yolk	

BAKING TINS

Two 18.5cm (7¼in) square sandwich tins greased and lined.

BAKING

Preheated oven, 180°C or 360°F or gas mark 4
Middle shelf
25 minutes or until golden brown

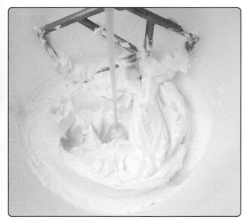

1. Cream the butter and sugar until light and fluffy. Then beat in the egg, a little at a time.

2. Sift the flour over the mixture and fold in lightly, with a metal spoon.

3. Mix in the chopped pears and apricots. Divide the mixture equally between the two sandwich tins.

4. Scatter the chopped cherries and angelica over the mixture in one tin. Bake the cakes then turn out onto a wire tray until cold.

5. For the filling, beat the butter and icing sugar until soft and creamy. Add the kirsch and egg yolk and beat until pale in colour.

6. Sandwich the sponges together with the filling, then sprinkle the top lightly with caster sugar.

CARROT CAKE (PASSION CAKE)

Serves 12-16

WORCESTER HERBS

1. Mix together the grated carrot, oil, sugar, whisked eggs, syrup and vanilla essence until smooth.

2. Sift together the flour, bicarbonate of soda, baking powder, cinnamon, grated nutmeg and salt. Then mix in the chopped walnuts and bran.

INGREDIENTS

Metric		Imperial
225g	Carrots, grated	8oz
170ml	Corn oil	6floz
170g	Light brown soft sugar	6oz
	3 eggs, size 3, whisked	
30ml	Golden syrup	2tbsp
5ml	Vanilla essence	1tsp
170g	Plain flour	6oz
5ml	Bicarbonate of soda	1tsp
5ml	Baking powder	1tsp
5ml	Cinnamon	1tsp
2.5ml	Grated nutmeg	½tsp
5ml	Salt	1tsp
115g	Walnut pieces, roughly chopped	4oz
28g	Bran	1oz

FILLING AND TOPPING

115g	Butter	4oz
225g	Icing sugar, sifted	8oz
115g	Philadelphia cream cheese or low fat soft cheese	4oz
2.5ml	Vanilla essence	½tsp

DECORATION

Whole pecan nuts
Sugarpaste carrots

BAKING TIN

21.5cm (8½in) round cake tin lined with greaseproof paper and greased.

BAKING

Preheated oven, 180°C or 360°F or gas mark 4
Middle shelf
1¼ hours

Mary's Tips

Cold eggs can cause mixtures to curdle. Before use, place whole eggs in hand-hot water for about 5 minutes to allow them to warm through.

3. Stir in the carrot mixture then beat well. Pour mixture into the tin and bake. After baking leave in tin for 5 minutes then turn out onto a wire tray until cold.

4. For the filling, cream the butter and icing sugar until smooth. Beat in the cheese and essence until light and fluffy.

5. Cut and fill the centre, then coat the top, using a combed scraper or fork. Decorate with pecan nuts and sugarpaste carrots.

GOLDEN BRAN CAKE

Serves 10-12

Mary's Tips

Cut into thin slices and spread lightly with butter for best eating results.

Eat within 5 days.

Freezes.

INGREDIENTS

Metric		Imperial
170g	Self raising flour	6oz
85g	Butter or margarine	3oz
57g	Natural bran	2oz
85g	Light brown soft sugar	3oz
5ml	Mixed spice	1tsp
	2 eggs, size 2, beaten	
30ml	Golden syrup	2 level tbsp
85g	Sultanas	3oz
150ml	Milk, approximately	¼pt

BAKING TIN

905g (2lb) loaf tin greased and base lined.

BAKING

Preheated oven, 180°C or 360°F or gas mark 4
Middle shelf
60 minutes or until firm when pressed in the centre. Leave in the tin to cool, before placing on a wire tray.

1. Sift the flour into a bowl, then rub in the butter or margarine. Stir in the bran, sugar and spice.

2. Add the eggs, syrup and sultanas with sufficient milk to form a fairly soft mixture.

3. Place mixture into the tin and sprinkle the top with a light layer of bran. Bake.

CHERRY and ALMOND CAKE

Serves 10-12

1. Cut cherries in half, wash and drain, leave to dry on a tea-towel overnight. Sift flours together into a bowl then mix in the ground almonds and cherries.

2. Beat the margarine, butter and sugar together until light and fluffy. Beat in the eggs a little at a time. Blend the mixtures together, using a spoon.

3. Spoon mixture into tin, and place chopped cherries and almonds on top. When baked leave in tin for 10 minutes then place cake on a wire tray until cold.

INGREDIENTS

Metric		Imperial
225g	Glacé cherries	8oz
145g	Self raising flour	5oz
57g	Plain flour	2oz
35g	Cornflour	1¼oz
35g	Ground almonds	1¼oz
85g	Margarine	3oz
85g	Butter	3oz
170g	Caster sugar	6oz
	3 eggs, size 3	

TOPPING

28g	Flaked almonds	1oz
28g	Cherries, chopped and washed	1oz

BAKING TIN

16.5cm (6½in) round cake tin greased and lined with greaseproof paper and lightly greased.

BAKING

Preheated oven, 180°C or 360°F or gas mark 4
Middle shelf
1-1½ hours

Mary's Tips

Glacé cherries often come in an over-sticky, sweet syrup, which is the reason they need washing and drying before use.

ALL-IN-ONE SWISS ROLL

Serves 10-12

LAVINIA

1. Place all the ingredients into a bowl and beat until light and creamy.

2. Pour the mixture into the tin and spread evenly, using a trowel shaped palette knife and bake.

3. Place a moist tea-towel onto table, then greaseproof paper on top covered with caster sugar. When baked turn out sponge immediately onto sugared paper.

INGREDIENTS

Metric		Imperial
85g	Soft margarine	3oz
170g	Caster sugar	6oz
	3 eggs, size 2	
170g	Self raising flour	6oz
	FILLING	
57g	Jam, warmed	2oz

BAKING TIN

33 x 23cm (13 x 9in) swiss roll tin, greased and lined with greaseproof paper, then greased.

BAKING

Preheated oven, 200°C or 390°F or gas mark 6
Middle shelf
10-12 minutes

Mary's Tips

The classic all-in-one swiss roll is quick and easy to make once the technique of rolling the hot sponge is mastered.

Swiss roll is often made with butter. If you do not intend to eat it all on the first day butter helps to keep it moister for longer.

Waste no time once the sponge is cooked. If you are slow the edges will go crisp as they cool – making the sponge crack as you roll.

The following variations suggest combinations of flavours, fillings and coatings.

1. CHOCOLATE ROLL

Substitute 30ml (2tbsp) of flour with 30ml (2tbsp) of cocoa powder, and follow the same recipe and method as below. Fill the roll with chocolate buttercream, whipped cream or ice-cream just before serving.

2. GINGER CREAM ROLL

Make according to basic recipe, but fill it with 300ml (½pt) whipped double cream mixed with 45ml (3tbsp) ginger wine and 30ml (2tbsp) finely chopped crystallised ginger. Use the excess to cover the outside of the roll and decorate with crystallised ginger.

3. WALNUT AND ORANGE ROLL

Make according to basic recipe, but add the grated rind of one orange to the mixture. Cook and leave to cool, rolled up, then finely chop 115g (4oz) walnuts. Beat 15-30ml (1-2tbsp) of honey into 115g (4oz) soft cheese. Stir in the nuts and fill the cake with the mixture.

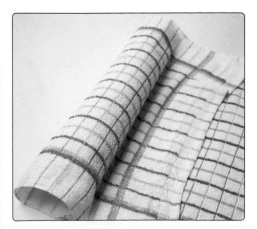

4. Remove the greaseproof paper the sponge was baked in, then immediately roll up the sponge and leave for 5 minutes to cool.

5. Carefully unroll the sponge and spread the filling evenly on top.

6. Roll up again, without the sugared paper or towel, and leave to cool on a wire tray.

ORANGE SEED CAKE

Serves 12-16

SANDRINGHAM

1. Cream the margarine until soft. Add the sugar and beat until light and fluffy. Thoroughly beat in the eggs, one at a time.

2. Stir in the seeds, milk and orange rind. Sift together the flour and baking powder and fold into the creamed mixture, alternately with orange juice.

3. Spoon the mixture into the prepared tin and bake. After baking leave to cool for 5 minutes then turn out onto a wire tray to cool. Dust with icing sugar.

INGREDIENTS

Metric		Imperial
170g	Block margarine	6oz
170g	Caster sugar	6oz
	3 eggs, size 3	
15ml	Caraway seeds	1tbsp
15ml	Milk	1tbsp
	Grated rind and juice of 1 orange	
225g	Plain flour	8oz
7.5ml	Baking powder	1½ level tsp
	Icing sugar for decoration	

BAKING TIN

21.5cm (8½in) brioche tin, well greased.

BAKING

Preheated oven, 170°C or 340°F or gas mark 4
Middle shelf
45 minutes

BUTTERMILK CHEESECAKE

Serves 16

1. *BASE. Mix the crumbled biscuits and sugar together then blend in the melted butter. Press mixture into the tin to cover base and a little up the side.*

2. *FILLING. Mix the egg, sugar and essence together then beat into the cream cheese. Stir in cream and buttermilk to make mixture a thick batter consistency.*

3. *Fold in the melted butter. Pour mixture into tin and bake. After baking leave in tin until cold. Chill before removing from tin, decorate and serve.*

ROYAL GARDEN

INGREDIENTS

Metric		Imperial
	BASE	
	8 digestive biscuits, crumbled	
15ml	Light brown soft sugar	1tbsp
57g	Butter, melted	2oz
	FILLING	
	3 eggs, size 3, lightly beaten	
170g	Caster sugar	6oz
5ml	Vanilla essence	1tsp
680g	Cream cheese	1½lb
225ml	Sour cream	8oz
225ml	Buttermilk	8oz
57g	Butter	2oz

BAKING TIN

21.5cm (8½in) round loose-bottomed cake tin, base lined.

BAKING

Preheated oven, 160°C or 320°F or gas mark 2½
Middle shelf
45-60 minutes

DECORATION

Fresh cream, whipped
Fresh fruit

LEMON and CHOCOLATE LAYER CAKE

Serves 8-10

SUMMERFIELD

1. Sift together the flour, salt and baking powder. Rub in the margarine.

2. Add the sugar, egg, lemon rind and milk.

3. Stir the mixture with a wooden spoon until a soft dropping consistency is reached.

26

4. *Spoon one third of the mixture into the tin, then sprinkle on some of the grated chocolate, as shown.*

INGREDIENTS

Metric		Imperial
340g	Plain flour	12oz
	Pinch of salt	
15ml	Baking powder	3tsp
130g	Margarine	4½oz
130g	Caster sugar	4½oz
	2 eggs, size 4	
	Grated lemon rind	3tsp
2ml	Milk	7oz
170g	Plain chocolate or cooking chocolate, finely chopped or grated	6oz

TOPPING

Icing sugar

BAKING TIN

18cm (7in) round cake tin greased and base lined with greased greaseproof paper.

BAKING

Preheated oven, 190°C or 370°F or gas mark 5 for 15 minutes, then reduce heat to 180°C or 350°F or gas mark 4 for one hour. Middle shelf.

Mary's Tips

Plain chocolate gives a better taste than cooking chocolate in this recipe. Real chocolate chips are now widely available for cake-making and can be chopped more finely, rather than grating a block.

Salt is a key ingredient in this, as in many other recipes. Without it, cakes can be flavourless. It also makes the gluten in the flour more elastic, thereby helping the mixture to rise.

5. *Spoon half the remaining mixture on top, then add more grated chocolate.*

6. *Spoon remaining mixture on top then, finally, sprinkle on the remaining grated chocolate.*

7. *Bake as recommended. When baked, leave in the tin for 30 minutes. Then remove from tin and leave to cool on a wire tray.*

8. *Using a fine sieve, dust the top lightly with icing sugar.*

SIMNEL CAKE

Serves 16

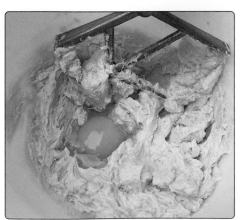

1. *Cream the butter and sugar together until light and fluffy. Thoroughly beat in the eggs, one at a time.*

2. *Mix the remaining dry ingredients together, then fold into the creamed butter, adding milk to make soft mixture. Spoon half the mixture into the tin.*

3. *Roll out the almond paste and place into the tin, then fill with remaining mixture. Slightly hollow the top. After baking leave in the tin for 30 minutes.*

INGREDIENTS

Metric		Imperial
225g	Plain wholemeal flour	8oz
170g	Light brown soft sugar	6oz
170g	Butter	6oz
	3 eggs, size 3	
170g	Sultanas	6oz
115g	Currants	4oz
57g	Peel	2oz
57g	Glacé cherries	2oz
2.5ml	Mixed spice	½tsp
1.25ml	Cinnamon	¼tsp
57g	Ground almonds	2oz
	Grated rind of 1 lemon	
	Grated rind of 1 small orange	
	Milk as required	

CAKE CENTRE

115g	Almond paste or marzipan	4oz

TOP DECORATION

Boiled apricot jam
340g (12oz) almond paste or marzipan
85g (3oz) sugarpaste
Royal icing for piping
Various food colours

GUM ARABIC SOLUTION

45ml (1½oz) water
15g (½oz) gum arabic powder
Boil the water, remove from heat and whisk in the powder. Leave to cool.

BAKING TIN

16.5cm (6in) round cake tin greased and lined with greaseproof paper.

BAKING

Preheated oven, 160°C or 320°F or gas mark 2½ for 1 hour then reduce heat to 150°C or 300°F or gas mark 2 for further 2-2½ hours
Middle shelf

4. *Remove baking paper and place cake onto a wire tray until cold. Brush top with boiling apricot jam. Mould almond paste balls and place around cake edge.*

5. *Make gum arabic solution. Place cake under a grill to colour the almond paste. Then immediately brush almond paste with gum arabic solution.*

6. *When the cake is cold, roll out the sugarpaste and cut into a fluted disc and place onto the cake-top.*

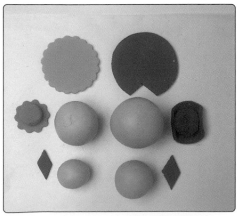

7. *Mould the various chicken shapes shown from sugarpaste or almond paste.*

8. *Fix the pieces together and decorate with piping and bows.*

9. *Fix the chickens and then pipe appropriate inscription.*

ALL-IN-ONE VICTORIA SANDWICH CAKE

Serves 12

ENGLISH GARDEN   MAYFIELD

Mary's Tips

A few drops of vanilla essence can be added for a different taste.

FILLING

Raspberry jam
Buttercream (see p.5)

INGREDIENTS

Metric		Imperial
285g	Self raising flour	10oz
12.5ml	Baking powder	2½tsp
285g	Soft margarine	10oz
285g	Caster sugar	10oz
	5 eggs, size 3	

TOPPING

Icing sugar

BAKING TINS

Two 21.5cm (8½in) round sandwich tins greased and floured.

BAKING

Preheated oven, 170°C or 340°F or gas mark 3
Middle shelf
35-45 minutes

1. Thoroughly sift the self raising flour and baking powder together, then place all the ingredients into a bowl.

2. Beat on slow speed, or by hand with a wooden spoon, until well mixed.

3. Divide the mixture equally into the tins and gently spread level. Bake. Turn out onto a wire tray to cool. Sandwich together then dust top with icing sugar.

GOLDEN SYRUP CAKE

Serves 8-10

Mary's Tips

This cake freezes
particularly well,
but don't sprinkle it with
the demerara sugar until
it is defrosted. Eat within
3 days if fresh, or after
defrosting.

INGREDIENTS

Metric		Imperial
225g	Margarine	8oz
115g	Demerara sugar	4oz
115ml	Golden syrup	4oz
	4 eggs, size 2	
225g	Self raising flour	8oz
	TOPPING	
15g	Demerara sugar	½oz

BAKING TIN

16.5cm (6½in) round cake tin greased
and base lined.

BAKING

Preheated oven, 180°C or 360°F or
gas mark 4
Middle shelf
55 minutes or until cooked

1. Cream the margarine, sugar and
syrup together until light and fluffy.

2. Thoroughly beat in the egg, a little at
a time. Sift and gently fold in the flour.

3. Spoon mixture into the tin. Bake.
When baked leave for 10 minutes. Turn
out onto a wire tray. Sprinkle top with
demerara sugar.

UNCOOKED CHOCOLATE CAKE

Serves 16-20

1. Roughly crush biscuits, then chop walnuts and mix together. Cream butter, sugar and syrup together. Beat in cocoa then mix in the biscuits.

2. Press evenly into the flan ring. Cover and leave overnight in a refrigerator.

3. After cooling cake overnight make the topping and spread over top, using a fork. Fix walnuts around the edge and sprinkle chocolate over the centre.

INGREDIENTS

Metric		Imperial
115g	Sweet biscuits	4oz
57g	Digestive biscuits	2oz
57g	Walnuts	2oz
100g	Butter or margarine	3½oz
28g	Caster sugar	1oz
85g	Golden syrup	3oz
57g	Cocoa powder, sifted	2oz
	TOPPING	
115ml	Milk chocolate	4oz
15ml	Hot water	1tbsp
57g	Butter	2oz
170g	Icing sugar, sifted	6oz

CAKE TIN

Grease a 20.5cm (8in) flan ring and place onto a flat serving dish or board.

TO MAKE THE TOPPING

Slowly heat the chocolate, water and butter together in a saucepan until all melted. Then beat in the icing sugar.

Mary's Tips

A mixture of dark and white chocolate, grated, with whole walnuts round the edge, makes very effective decoration

COCONUT CAKE

Serves 10-14

WORCESTER HERBS

INGREDIENTS

Metric		Imperial
145g	Butter or margarine	5oz
170g	Caster sugar	6oz
	2 eggs, size 2	
45ml	Milk	3tbsp
225g	Self raising flour, sifted	8oz
115g	Dessicated coconut	4oz

TOPPING

115g	Philadelphia cheese	4oz
28g	Butter	1oz
170g	Icing sugar, sifted	6oz

DECORATION

Toasted flaked coconut

BAKING TIN

905g (2lb) loaf tin greased and base lined.

BAKING

Preheated oven, 170°C or 340°F or gas mark 3
Middle shelf
1½ hours.

1. Cream the butter and sugar until light and fluffy. Beat together the egg and milk. Add slowly to the creamed butter and sugar, beating well.

2. Slowly fold in the flour and coconut, using a metal spoon, until clear. Spoon mixture into tin and bake. After baking remove from tin when cold.

3. Beat all the ingredients for the topping together, until pale and creamy in colour. Then pipe onto the cake-top. Sprinkle with toasted coconut.

AUSTRIAN COFFEE CAKE

Serves 16-20

VICEROY GOLD

INGREDIENTS

Metric		Imperial
255g	Butter	9oz
225g	Caster sugar	8oz
	4 eggs, size 2, separated	
5ml	Grated lemon rind	1tsp
28g	Vanilla sugar	1oz
285g	Plain flour	10oz
5ml	Baking powder	1tsp

SOAKING MIXTURE

255g (9 fl oz) strong black coffee, cold.
Soft light brown sugar to taste
Brandy to taste

COATING

285g (10oz) whipping cream
Coffee flavouring
85g (3oz) toasted flaked almonds
Coffee powder for dusting

BAKING TIN

21.5cm (8½in) round cake tin greased and fully lined.

BAKING

Preheated oven, 180°C or 360°F or gas mark 4
Middle shelf
1¼ hours

1. Beat together the butter and caster sugar until light and fluffy. Thoroughly beat in the egg yolks, one at a time. Then mix in the grated lemon rind.

2. Sift the flour and baking powder together. Whisk the egg whites with the vanilla sugar until stiff.

3. Lightly fold into the creamed butter, alternate spoonfuls of egg white and flour until well blended. Place in tin and bake. When baked, leave in tin for 10 minutes.

4. Turn out onto a wire tray to cool. Mix cold coffee with sugar and brandy to taste. Place cake back into tin, prick top with skewer and brush on liquid.

5. Leave to soak for 2 hours. Whip the cream and flavour with coffee. Remove cake from tin and coat top and side with the cream.

6. Sprinkle toasted flaked almonds onto the cake top then cover the sides. Dust the top with cocoa powder. Chill and serve.

CHOCOLATE and ORANGE CAKE

Serves 8-10

1. Beat the butter and sugar until light and fluffy. Then mix in the grated orange and lemon rind.

2. Stir in the chocolate powder and ground almonds then beat well again. Whisk the eggs in a separate bowl until well mixed.

3. Beat the eggs into the mixture a little at a time, add a tablespoon of the flour and the brandy if required. Fold in remaining flour using a spatula, or spoon.

INGREDIENTS

Metric		Imperial
115g	Butter	4oz
115g	Caster sugar	4oz
	Grated rind of ½ an orange	
	Grated rind of ½ a lemon	
57g	Drinking chocolate powder	2oz
115g	Ground almonds	4oz
	2 eggs, size 2	
57g	Self raising flour, sifted	2oz
10ml	Brandy – optional	1dsp

SUGGESTED FILLINGS

Apricot jam
Orange or lemon curd
Raspberry jam

CHOCOLATE FUDGE ICING

115g (4oz) plain or milk chocolate
57g (2oz) unsalted butter
1 egg, size 3, beaten
170g (6oz) icing sugar, sifted

Mary's Tips

Variations on chocolate fudge icing include:

- adding finely chopped walnuts
- adding 30ml (2tbsp) rum
- adding grated orange rind
- using 15ml (1tbsp) honey instead of 25g (1oz) of sugar
- adding 5ml (1tsp) of instant coffee granules
- adding a pinch of ground ginger plus 30ml (2tbsp) of chopped stem ginger

BAKING TIN

905g (2lb) loaf tin, greased and base lined.

BAKING

Preheated oven, 160°C or 320°F or gas mark 2½
Middle shelf
¾-1 hour

4. *Spoon mixture into tin and bake. After baking leave for 20 minutes then turn out onto a wire tray to cool. Slice and fill, then coat with boiled apricot jam.*

5. *For topping, melt the chocolate and butter together, then stir in the beaten egg. Remove from heat, then stir in the icing sugar and beat well.*

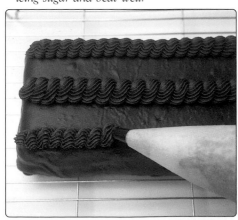

6. *When topping is slightly cooled, spread over the cake-top and sides. Pipe remaining topping as shown then decorate as required.*

CARAMEL SANDWICH CAKE

Serves 8

BEAUFORT

INGREDIENTS

Metric		Imperial
115g	Butter or margarine	4oz
115g	Granulated sugar	4oz
	2 eggs, size 3	
57g	Cube sugar	2oz
150ml	Hot milk	¼pt
170g	Plain flour, sifted	6oz
2.5ml	Baking powder	½tsp
	Apricot jam	
	Icing sugar	

BAKING TIN

Two 19cm (7½in) round sandwich tins, greased and floured.

BAKING

Preheated oven, 190°C or 375°F or gas mark 5 for about 30 minutes.

Mary's Tips

When making caramel, allow the sugar to dissolve slowly over a gentle heat, without stirring, until it has turned brown.

1. *Cream together the butter or margarine and the sugar until light. Separate eggs, and beat in the yolks.*

2. *Make a caramel by heating the loaf sugar in a small pan until it melts and turns light brown. Cool slightly.*

3. *Add the hot milk carefully and stir until the caramel is dissolved.*

4. *When caramel mixture is lukewarm, add it gradually to the creamed ingredients, and beat together.*

5. *Stir in the sieved dry ingredients and mix well, adding a little more milk if necessary. The mixture should be of soft dropping consistency.*

6. *Stiffly beat the egg whites and fold them in. Place in tins and bake as above. Fill the cooled cake with apricot jam and sprinkle the top with icing sugar.*

INGREDIENTS

Metric		Imperial
	4 eggs, size 3	
115g	Caster sugar	4oz
115g	Plain flour	4oz
	few drops of almond essence	
31g	Melted butter	1¼oz
	FILLING	
300ml	Double cream	10fl.oz
30ml	Amaretto liqueur	2tbsp
	1 small can mandarin oranges	
	2 kiwi fruit, sliced	

BAKING TIN

32.5cm x 23cm (13 x 9in) swiss roll tin, greased and lined with greased greaseproof paper.

BAKING

Preheated oven at 200°C or 400°F or gas mark 6, for 8-10 minutes.

Mary's Tips

Any fruit can be combined with cream for a filling, according to taste and season.

Freeze by rolling up the warm swiss roll with paper inside. Wrap in waxed paper when cool, then freeze for up to 6 months.

Fill with cream and fruit when fully defrosted.

1. Whisk the eggs, sugar and almond essence over a pan of hot water. Beat until mixture is light, creamy, double in bulk and shows the marks of the beaters.

2. Fold in the sifted flour carefully, and fold in the melted butter gently.

3. Pour into the prepared swiss roll tin and bake for 8-10 minutes.

4. Turn out onto a sheet of greaseproof paper sprinkled with caster sugar. Remove the paper which lined the tin.

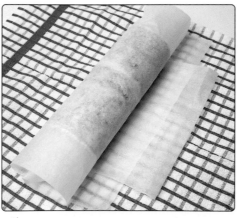

5. Lay a fresh piece of greaseproof paper on top, and carefully roll up the cake with the paper inside. Leave to cool.

6. For the filling, whisk the cream and liqueur to soft peaks, then fold in the chopped fruit, leaving a few pieces to decorate.

SWISS FRUIT ROLL

Serves 8

7. *Carefully unroll the cake, remove the paper, and spread evenly with the cream and fruit.*

8. *Roll up the cake again, and either sprinkle with caster sugar, or cover with more cream or butter icing, according to taste.*

9. *Decorate with remaining pieces of fruit.*

SAFFRON CAKE

Serves 10-12

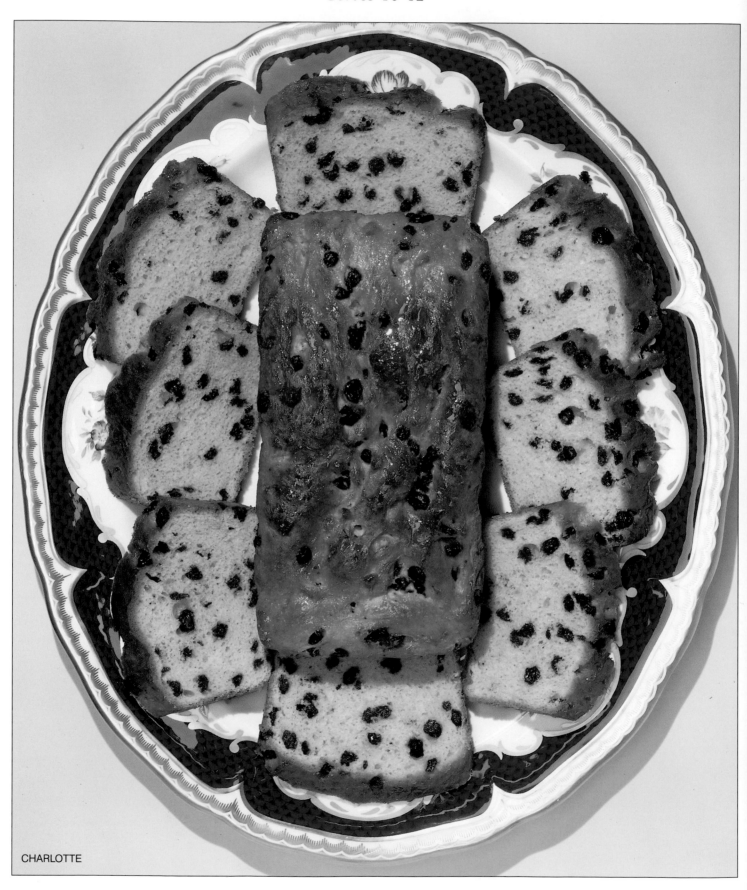

CHARLOTTE

INGREDIENTS

Metric		Imperial
150ml	Water	¼ pt
	Pinch of saffron strands	
150ml	Milk	¼ pt
15g	Dried yeast	½oz
	Pinch of sugar	
445g	Strong plain flour	1lb
5ml	Salt	1tsp
115g	Butter	4oz
170g	Currants	6oz
	Grated rind of ½ a lemon	
28g	Caster sugar	1oz

BAKING TINS

Two 905g (2lb) loaf tins greased and base lined.

BAKING

Preheated oven, 200°C or 390°F or gas mark 6 for 15 minutes then reduce heat to 180°C or 360°F or gas mark 4 for further 15-20 minutes Middle shelf
Do not open the door during the baking.

Mary's Tips

This is a variation of the traditional Cornish saffron bread, which like this, is a rich golden-yellow colour from the saffron strands.

1. Boil the water, add saffron, remove heat and soak overnight. Warm the milk, add yeast and pinch of sugar, leave in a warm place for 15 minutes until frothy.

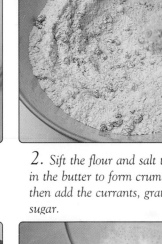

2. Sift the flour and salt together. Rub in the butter to form crumbly mixture then add the currants, grated rind and sugar.

3. Strain the saffron liquid into a saucepan and discard the strands. Warm slightly then mix into the dry ingredients.

4. Add the milk and yeast mixture and beat well to form a dough.

5. Divide the mixture between the two tins, cover with a cloth and leave in a warm place for 1 hour.

6. After 1 hour, or when the mixture has risen to ⅔rds the height of the tin, bake in the oven. When baked remove from tin and leave to cool on a wire tray.

DUNDEE CAKE

Serves 8-10

1. *Dissolve the bicarbonate of soda in the water, pour into a saucepan and add the butter, sugar and fruits. Bring to boil on low heat then simmer for 15 minutes.*

2. *Remove from heat and leave to cool completely. Add the rum. Beat the eggs until frothy then add to the mixture.*

3. *Sift the flour and baking powder together then fold into the mixture with the syrup and marmalade, using a metal spoon.*

INGREDIENTS

Metric		Imperial
5ml	Bicarbonate of soda	1tsp
60ml	Water	2fl.oz
115g	Butter or margarine	4oz
200g	Caster sugar	7oz
115g	Dried apricots, chopped	4oz
370g	Sultanas	13oz
60ml	Dark rum	4tbsp
	2 eggs, size 2	
225g	Strong plain flour, sifted	8oz
10ml	Baking powder	2tsp
15ml	Golden syrup	1tbsp
15ml	Marmalade	1 heaped tbsp
	TOPPING	
57g	Blanched almonds, split in half	2oz
30ml	Milk	2tbsp
57g	Caster sugar	1oz

BAKING TIN

16.5cm (6½in) round cake tin greased and lined.

BAKING

Preheated oven, 170°C or 340°F or gas mark 3
Middle shelf
1¼ hours

BAKING TEST

Test cake with a skewer after 1¼ hours, if uncooked at this time reduce heat to 150°C or 300°F or gas mark 2 and cook until baked. When cooked, cool in the tin for 15 minutes, then turn out and leave to cool on a wire tray.

Mary's Tips

If you prefer the topping almonds not too brown, then remove the cake from the oven half way through and scatter them on, brushing with milk and sugar immediately. They will be less neatly arranged, but paler in colour on the finished cake.

The Dundee Cake is one of the most difficult to test for readiness. I recommend sticking the skewer down between the cake and the tin to warm the skewer. A warm skewer will give a better indication once it is stuck into the centre of the cake. If the skewer comes out quite clean – the cake is ready. If not, test after a further 10-15 minutes.

4. Place the almonds into a small bowl and cover with the milk. Leave for two minutes.

5. Spoon the cake mixture into the tin and level.

6. From the centre place the drained almonds in tight circles around cake-top. Sprinkle the top with milk then with caster sugar. Bake as recommended.

DATE and SPICE CAKE

Serves 8-10

1. *Beat the butter until soft, then add the sugar and beat mixture until light and fluffy. Add the eggs, one at a time, beating well between each addition.*

2. *Sift together the flour, salt, baking powder and mixed spice into a bowl. Stir two tablespoons of this mixture into the ~~tes~~.*

INGREDIENTS

Metric		Imperial
225g	Butter	8oz
225g	Caster sugar	8oz
	3 eggs, size 2	
225g	Sugar rolled chopped dates	8oz
285g	Plain flour	10oz
2.5ml	Baking powder	1 level tsp
	Pinch of salt	
5ml	Mixed spice	2 level tsp

BAKING TIN

25.5cm (10in) round fluted cake tin, well greased and base lined.

BAKING

Preheated ove ~~360°F or gas mar~~ minutes then reduce ~~160°C or 320°F or ga~~ 3 for approximately 1½ ~~s.~~ When baked leave in the for 30 minutes then turn out onto a wire tray.

Mary's Tips

This can also be made in a 20cm (8in) round tin or an 18cm (7in) square tin, greased and lined.

3. *Using a metal spoon, blend all ingredients together into the creamed mixture. Place into the tin, slightly hollow out the centre and bake.*

PINEAPPLE UPSIDE-DOWN CAKE

Serves 8-12

POPPIES

1. Brush the syrup over the greaseproof paper in the tin, then sprinkle on the brown sugar. Strain the pineapple rings and place the rings in the tin.

2. Whisk the eggs and sugar until light and fluffy. Sift the flour and gently fold into the mixture. Pour mixture into tin and bake.

3. After baking leave in the tin for 15 minutes, upturn and carefully turn out onto a wire tray to cool. Decorate with cherries and angelica.

INGREDIENTS

Metric		Impe...
30ml	Golden syrup	**1oz**
28g	Light brown soft sugar	**1oz**
340g	Can of pineapple rings	**12oz**
	3 eggs, size 2	
85g	Caster sugar	**3oz**
85g	Plain flour	**3oz**

DECORATION

Glacé cherries, cut in half
Angelica, cut into diamonds

...KING TIN

21.5cm (8½in) round sponge tin greased with butter, base lined with greaseproof paper and greased with more butter.

BAKING

Preheated oven, 180°C or 360°F or gas mark 4
Middle shelf
40-45 minutes.

1. *Sift together the flour, cocoa powder and baking powder. Whisk the egg yolks and sugar together until stiff.*

2. *Fold in the ground walnuts. Whisk the egg whites until stiff then fold in. Add the hot water and fold in.*

INGREDIENTS

Metric		Imperial
90g	Plain flour	3¼oz
21g	Cocoa powder	¾oz
3ml	Baking powder	½ heaped tsp
	5 eggs, size 2 separated	
145g	Caster sugar	5oz
115g	Ground walnuts	4oz
40ml	Hot water	4dsp

TOPPING

85g	Caster sugar	3oz
300ml	Double cream	½pt
	Walnuts	
	Chocolate pieces	

BAKING TIN

33 x 23cm (13 x 9in) swiss roll tin, greased and lined with greaseproof paper, then greased.

BAKING

Preheated oven, 180°C or 360°F or gas mark 4
Middle shelf
20 minutes

Mary's Tips

This makes a denser, richer swiss roll than the ordinary fatless one, and therefore makes a perfect dinner party pudding.

Ensure you chill the cream before whisking. A hand (balloon & spiral) whisk gives good results but involves hard work. Avoid using a large electric beater as it is easy to overwhip the cream. Remember to use a big bowl to provide plenty of space for introducing air into the cream.

Whipped cream freezes well by itself in a rigid covered container for up to 4 months. However, once the whipped cream is applied to the cake it should be consumed that day.

3. *Fold in the sieved ingredients. Spread evenly into the tin and bake. Lay a piece of greaseproof paper on a damp tea-towel and sprinkle with caster sugar.*

4. *When baked turn out onto the paper and immediately roll up. Leave on a wire tray until cold.*

5. *Whisk the cream until firm. Unroll the sponge and spread most of the cream on top.*

WALNUT ROLL

Serves 10-12

6. *Sprinkle chopped walnuts over the cream.*

7. *Gently roll up the sponge and sprinkle top with caster sugar if required. Place onto the serving dish or plate.*

8. *Pipe remaining cream on top and decorate with walnuts and pieces of chocolate.*

BATTENBURG
Serves 8-12

INGREDIENTS

Metric		Imperial
225g	Butter or margarine	8oz
225g	Caster sugar	8oz
	4 eggs, size 3, lightly beaten	
225g	Plain flour, sifted	8oz
5ml	Baking powder	1tsp
	Pink food colouring	
	Almond essence	
	Vanilla essence	

FILLING

Raspberry seedless jam

COVERING

225g	Marzipan	8oz
	Caster sugar for rolling	
	Apricot purée	
	Glacé cherries	
	Angelica	

BAKING TINS

Two 905g (2lb) loaf tins greased and base lined.

BAKING

Preheated oven, 180°C or 360°F or gas mark 4
Middle shelf
40-45 minutes

Mary's Tips

Go gently with the colouring for this recipe. The pink can be a very light shade to achieve the desired effect. Bakers often use a hard pink in the shops to attract the eye but it is not necessary in the home produced cake.

1. Beat the butter and sugar together until light and fluffy. Then thoroughly beat in the egg, a little at a time.

2. Sift the flour and baking powder together and blend into the batter, using a spoon, until clear.

3. Divide the mixture by weight, in half into separate bowls. Mix pink colour and almond essence in one, then vanilla into the other. Place into tins and bake.

4. When baked turn out onto a wire tray to cool. Then trim the sides, cut into strips and layer with the jam filling.

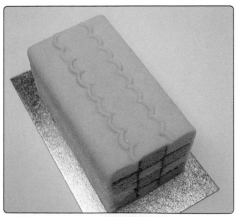

5. Roll out the marzipan, using caster sugar as dusting. Warm apricot purée, brush onto marzipan and wrap around cake. Crimp a pattern on the top.

6. Decorate with cherries and angelica diamonds.

51

WINE FRUIT CAKE

Serves 16-20

JACOBEAN FLORAL

Mary's Tips

This cake can be wrapped in waxed paper and stored in a cupboard for up to 3 months.

Very good quality cake which can be eaten on its own or used for special occasions such as a wedding.

INGREDIENTS

Metric		Imperial
170g	Block margarine	6oz
120ml	Golden syrup	8 level tbsp
285g	Seedless raisins	10oz
225g	Currants	8oz
145g	Sultanas	5oz
145g	Cut mixed peel	5oz
85g	Glacé cherries, cut into quarters	3oz
200ml	Red table wine	7oz
	3 eggs, size 2	
285g	Plain flour	10oz

1 rounded tsp mixed spice, 1 level tsp nutmeg
Pinch of salt, ½tsp bicarbonate of soda

BAKING TIN

20.5cm (8in) round or 18cm (7in) square deep tin greased with white fat, then lined with greaseproof paper then the paper greased.

BAKING

Preheated oven, 140°C or 285°F or gas mark 1
Centre of oven
1¾-2 hours

1. Place margarine, syrup, fruit and wine into a saucepan over gentle heat. Stir until margarine has melted. Bring to boil and gently cook for 5 minutes.

2. Pour the mixture into a bowl. When cold beat in the eggs. Sift together the flour, spice, nutmeg, salt and bicarbonate of soda into a mixing bowl.

3. Add fruit mixture to flour and mix well. Place in tin, level the top and bake. When baked leave in tin for 30 minutes before turning out onto a wire tray.

MIXED FRUIT TEABREAD

Serves 8

FORGET-ME-NOT

Mary's Tips

Double the recipe and divide between four 445g (1lb) loaf tins.

Freezes well.

This is a very moist teabread and can be eaten without butter. Best eaten 1-2 days after baking.

INGREDIENTS

Metric		Imperial
170g	Raisins	6oz
115g	Sultanas	4oz
57g	Currants	2oz
115g	Light brown soft sugar	4oz
300ml	Cold tea	½pt
	1 egg, size 2, beaten	
45ml	Golden syrup	3tbsp
225g	Plain wholemeal flour	8oz
7.5ml	Baking powder	1½ level tsp
2.5ml	Mixed spice	½ level tsp

BAKING TIN

905g (2lb) loaf tin greased and base lined.

BAKING

Preheated oven, 170°C or 340°F or gas mark 3
Middle shelf
30 minutes then
cover loosely with foil
bake for further 40-60 minutes.

1. Soak the fruit and sugar in the cold tea for 12 hours.

2. Beat in the egg and the syrup. Sift the flour, baking powder and mixed spice together.

3. Fold into the mixture and mix well. Spoon into the tins. Bake in preheated oven following instructions. Cool on a wire tray. Wrap in foil when cold.

SOUR CREAM and NUT CAKE

Serves 10

1. *Cream the butter and sugar until light and fluffy. Thoroughly beat in the egg a little at a time. Then beat in the sour cream.*

2. *Sift together the flour, salt, baking powder and soda, then beat into the creamed mixture to form a smooth batter.*

INGREDIENTS

Metric		Imperial
90g	Butter	3¼oz
80g	Caster sugar	2¾oz
	1 egg, size 3, lightly beaten	
7ml	Sour cream	2½oz
145g	Plain flour	5oz
	Pinch of salt	
5ml	Baking powder	1tsp
1.25ml	Baking soda	¼tsp
	Vanilla flavour	

FILLING AND TOPPING

50g	Caster sugar	1¾oz
2.5ml	Cinnamon	½tsp
30g	Toasted almonds	1oz

BAKING TIN

21.5cm (8½in) brioche tin, well greased.

BAKING

Preheated oven, 160°C or 320°F or gas mark 2½
Middle shelf
45-50 minutes

Mary's Tips

Make sure you leave enough topping for the final layer of the cake. If it looks short, scatter on a few extra flaked almonds, toasted.

When breaking eggs, I recommend the use of a teaspoon to remove any pieces of shell which could fall into the bowl. Try not to store eggs in the fridge in the trays. Eggs keep much better in their covered cartons.

3. *Mix all the filling and topping ingredients together in a separate bowl.*

4. *Place a ⅓rd of the batter into the tin, then sprinkle on a ⅓rd of the filling.*

5. *Spread ½ the remaining batter on top, then filling, then repeat again with remainders. After baking leave in tin until cold.*

VINE HARVEST

LEMON BANANA CAKE

Serves 10-12

1. Cream the butter until light and fluffy. Thoroughly beat in the sugar. Add the essence, beaten eggs and mashed bananas and mix well.

2. Sift together the flour, bicarbonate of soda and salt then blend into the mixture, with the sour milk, using a spoon.

3. Spread the mixture into the two tins evenly, using a palette knife. After baking leave in the tins for 5 minutes then turn out onto a wire tray until cold.

56

INGREDIENTS

Metric		Imperial
255g	Plain flour	9oz
2.5ml	Bicarbonate of soda	½tsp
	Pinch of salt	
115g	Butter or margarine	4oz
170g	Caster sugar	6oz
	A few drops of lemon essence	
	2 eggs, size 3, beaten	
	2 medium bananas, mashed	
150ml	Sour milk	¼pt

FILLING

57g	Butter	2oz
85g	Icing sugar	3oz
	Lemon curd	

TOPPING

15ml	Lemon juice	1tbsp
145g	Icing sugar	5oz
	Dried fruits	

BAKING TINS

Two 18.5cm (7¼in) round sandwich tins greased and base lined.

BAKING

Preheated oven, 190°C or 370°F or gas mark 5
Middle shelf
30 minutes

Mary's Tips

Ripe brown bananas are much better for cakes than unblemished yellow ones. Mash them with a fork or purée them in a blender or food processor.

Although this recipe can make use of ripe bananas. Be careful not to use old lemons for the juice. A very small amount can produce a wooden taste to the cake.

The lemon glacé icing provides an excellent sweet-sour taste to round off the cake. However, this icing will not retain its glossiness for long. I occasionally mix in some stock syrup to make it smooth and glossy.

4. For the filling, beat the butter and icing sugar until light and fluffy. Spread over one sponge then pipe the lemon curd and place other sponge on top.

5. For the topping, pour the lemon juice into a saucepan and stir in the icing sugar. Stir over heat until the icing is just warm to the touch.

6. Quickly spread the icing on top then decorate with the fruits.

SPICY PLUM AND SYRUP CAKE

Serves 16

INGREDIENTS

Metric		Imperial
445g	Self raising flour	1lb
	Pinch of salt	
5ml	Allspice	1tsp
115g	Soft light brown sugar	4oz
225g	Hard margarine	8oz
115g	Raisins	4oz
445g	Fresh plums	1lb
120ml	Golden syrup	8tbsp
	4 eggs, size 3	

TOPPING

45ml	Soft light brown sugar	3tbsp
5ml	Allspice	1tsp

BAKING TIN

21.5cm (8½in) round cake tin greased and fully lined.

BAKING

Preheated oven, 180°C or 360°F or gas mark 4
Middle shelf
1¼ hours

Wrap the cake in foil and keep for at least two days before eating.

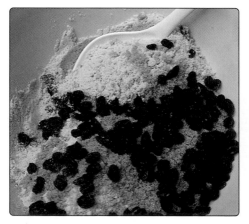

1. *Sift the flour, salt and spice into a mixing bowl. Cut margarine into pieces then rub into the flour to form a fine crumbly mix. Stir in sugar and raisins.*

2. *Cut plums in half, remove stones. Put 10-12 halves aside, chop remaining into small pieces. Beat the syrup and eggs together then blend into mixture with plums.*

3. *Spoon mixture into the tin and level. Place plum halves on top. Mix topping ingredients together and sprinkle on top then bake. Leave in the tin until cold.*

PARADISE CAKE

Serves 16-20

INGREDIENTS

Metric		Imperial
285g	Block margarine	10oz
285g	Light brown soft sugar	10oz
	5 eggs, size 2	
1.25ml	Almond essence	¼tsp
315g	Plain flour	11oz
2.5ml	Baking powder	½tsp
42g	Ground almonds	1½oz
145g	Glacé cherries, chopped	5oz
57g	Angelica, chopped	2oz
170g	Crystallised fruits, chopped	6oz

DECORATION

Wide selection of crystallised fruits as required.
Clear jelly.

BAKING

Preheated oven, 150°C or 300°F or gas mark 2
Middle shelf
Approximately 2½ hours

BAKING TIN

21.5cm (8½in) brioche tin, well greased.

1. Beat the margarine and sugar until light. Beat in the egg, a little at a time. Add the essence. Sift the flour and baking powder then fold into the mixture.

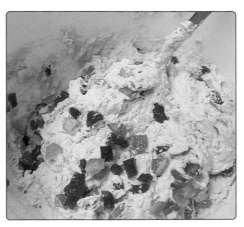

2. Fold in the ground almonds and chopped fruits. Mix until well blended. Place into tin. Bake, leave for 15 mins, then upturn onto a wire tray until cold.

3. When cold glaze the top with jelly, place crystallised fruits on top then cover with more jelly. Leave until set.

COFFEE SULTANA CAKE

Serves 16-20

INGREDIENTS

Metric		Imperial
145g	Butter or margarine	5oz
145g	Light brown soft sugar	5oz
	2 eggs, size 3	
20ml	Coffee extract	1½ tbsp
225g	Plain flour	8oz
2.5ml	Baking powder	½ tsp
115g	Sultanas	4oz
	Milk to mix	

TOPPING

Mixed chopped nuts
Pecan nuts

BAKING TIN

905g (2lb) loaf tin greased and base lined.

BAKING

Preheated oven, 190°C or 370°F or gas mark 5
Middle shelf
1-1¼ hours

PURPLE VINE

1. Cream the butter and sugar and thoroughly beat in the eggs a little at a time. Beat in the coffee extract.

2. Sift together the flour and baking powder. Stir into the mixture with the sultanas and sufficient milk to make a soft consistency.

3. Place mixture into the tin. Sprinkle with chopped nuts then place pecan nuts on top. After baking leave for 10 minutes then turn out onto a wire tray to cool.

HURRELL LOAF

Serves 16

CHINESE GARDEN

INGREDIENTS

Metric		Imperial
170g	Wholemeal plain flour	6oz
115g	Self raising flour	4oz
2.5ml	Baking powder	½ tsp
	Pinch of nutmeg	
170g	Sultanas	6oz
57g	Walnuts,	2oz
	Chopped	
115g	Demerara sugar	4oz
225ml	Black treacle	8oz
200ml	Milk	¼ pt plus 3 tbsp

BAKING TIN

905g (2lb) loaf tin, lightly greased and base lined.

BAKING

Preheated oven, 170°C or 340°F or gas mark 3
Middle shelf
1-1¼ hours

1. Put the wholemeal flour into a bowl, sift in the self-raising flour together with the baking powder and nutmeg. Stir in the sultanas, walnuts and sugar.

2. Pour the treacle into a saucepan, add the milk and stir over low heat until the liquids combine. Pour the liquid into the dry ingredients and mix well.

3. Spoon the mixture into the tin and bake. After baking leave in the tin for 15 minutes then turn out onto a wire tray to cool. Serve sliced and buttered.

1. *Sieve the flour, cornflour and baking powder into a mixing bowl. Rub in the margarine and stir in the sugar and sultanas.*

INGREDIENTS

Metric		Imperial
170g	Plain flour	6oz
57g	Cornflour	2oz
10ml	Baking powder	2tsp
115g	Light brown sugar	4oz
115g	Margarine	4oz
57g	Sultanas	2oz
	1 egg, size 3	
90ml	Milk	6tbsp

TOPPING

57g	Plain flour	2oz
57g	Demerara sugar	2oz
15ml	Cinnamon	1tbsp
28g	Margarine	1oz

BAKING TIN

21.5cm (8½in) sponge tin, greased.

BAKING

Preheated oven at 190°C or 375°F or gas mark 5, for 45 minutes.

Mary's Tips

This cake is most delicious when eaten while still warm.

Demerara sugar has about 2 per cent molasses in it. Dark brown Muscovado sugar has about 13 per cent molasses. Be wary of using Muscovado sugar on delicate cakes as the molasses will darken the colour and can alter the flavour. The soft, fine texture makes it ideal for fruit cakes.

2. *Mix to a soft dough with the beaten egg and milk.*

3. *Put the mixture into a greased sponge tin, and smooth over with a spatula.*

4. *Make the topping by rubbing the margarine into the flour, sugar and cinnamon.*

5. *Spoon this over the raw cake mixture and bake for about 45 minutes.*

CINNAMON CRUMBLE CAKE

Serves 10

WARMSTRY WHITE

APPLE GINGERBREAD RING

Serves 12-16

INGREDIENTS A

Metric		Imperial
225g	Plain flour	8oz
2.5ml	Salt	½tsp
7.5ml	Ground ginger	1½tsp
7.5ml	Baking powder	1½tsp
2.5ml	Bicarbonate of soda	½tsp

Step 1. Sift the ingredients listed in A together into a large bowl.

INGREDIENTS B

Metric		Imperial
115g	Light brown soft sugar	4oz
85g	Butter or margarine	3oz
28ml	Black treacle	1oz
115ml	Golden syrup	4oz

Step 2. Place all the ingredients listed in B into a saucepan and gently heat until the butter melts.

INGREDIENTS C

Metric		Imperial
150ml	Milk	¼pt
	1 egg, size 2	

Step 3. Pour the milk into a separate saucepan and warm slightly, remove from the heat, and beat in the egg.

GLAZE

57ml (2oz) golden syrup
150ml (½pt) water
2.5ml (½tsp) ground ginger
10ml (2tsp) arrowroot
30ml (2tbsp) preserved stem ginger syrup

For the glaze, pour the syrup and water into a saucepan, bring to the boil and simmer for 5 minutes. Blend together the ground ginger, arrowroot and ginger syrup in a separate bowl. Pour on the hot syrup, stir well and return to the pan. Continue boiling and stirring for 2 minutes.

FILLING

3 eating apples, cored, peeled, sliced and washed in lemon juice to stop browning
16 whole stoned dates
2 large pieces of preserved stem ginger, cut into thin strips.

BAKING TIN

20.5cm (8in) ring mould well greased.

BAKING

Preheated oven, 180°C or 360°F or gas mark 4
Middle shelf
35 minutes approximately

1. *Follow steps one to three in the ingredients listing then blend liquid mixtures into the dry ingredients, using a spoon.*

2. *Pour the mixture into the prepared tin and immediately place into the oven and bake.*

3. *When baked leave in the tin for 5 minutes then upturn onto a wire tray to cool.*

Mary's Tips

Plain flour is essential for this recipe. The raising agent in self raising flour would conflict with the bicarbonate of soda, which is necessary for the dark gingerbread colour.

I strongly recommend the mixture of Golden syrup and black treacle in B. Black treacle alone gives a bitter taste and golden syrup alone, an anaemic cake. If the cooked cake is doughy or sunk in the middle, you have probably used too much syrup.

MOUNTBATTEN BLUE

4. Follow the instructions for making the glaze.

5. Add the prepared sliced apples to the glaze and poach for 10-15 minutes, or until just tender.

6. Strain the apples and place into the centre of the cake with the dates and ginger. Then brush the glaze over the cake.

65

APPLE, DATE and COCONUT CAKE

Serves 8-10

MANOR HOUSE

Mary's Tips

It is best to use a dessert apple for this cake, rather than a cooker. I used Golden Delicious, but any variety will do. The cake can also be glazed with melted apricot jam if required. It is best eaten fresh, but does freeze well too.

INGREDIENTS

Metric		Imperial
285g	Self raising flour	10oz
57g	Desiccated coconut	2oz
115g	Dates, chopped	4oz
115g	Block margarine	4oz
60g	Trex	2oz
170g	Caster sugar	6oz
	1 medium sized apple	
	3 eggs, size 2	

BAKING TIN

16.5cm (6½in) round cake tin greased and fully lined with greaseproof paper.

BAKING

Preheated oven, 180°C or 360°F or gas mark 4
Middle shelf
1¾ hours

1. Sift the flour into a bowl then stir in the coconut. Add the chopped dates. Rub in the margarine and Trex until mixture resembles fine breadcrumbs.

2. Stir in sugar. Peel and core apple then chop half into small squares and add to mixture. Beat the eggs and stir into mixture to blend ingredients evenly.

3. Spoon into the tin. Slice remaining apple and place on top. After baking leave in tin to cool before removing.

ROSE MARBLED CAKE

Serves 14-16

VICEROY SILVER

INGREDIENTS

Metric		Imperial	Metric		
170g	Butter	6oz	57g	Ground almonds	2oz
170g	Caster sugar	6oz		A little milk if	
2.5ml	Almond essence	½tsp		necessary	
	3 eggs, size 3, lightly beaten			Food colouring of choice	
225g	Self raising flour sifted with a pinch of salt	8oz	15ml	Cocoa powder	1tbsp

BAKING TIN

16.5cm (6½in) round cake tin greased and lined.

BAKING

Preheated oven, 180°C or 360°F or gas mark 4
Middle shelf
50-60 minutes

1. Cream butter and sugar until light and fluffy, add essence. Beat in the eggs a little at a time. Fold in the flour and ground almonds, add milk if too stiff.

2. Divide the mixture into three equal parts. Leave one plain, colour the second with pink food colouring and add the cocoa powder to the third.

3. Place alternate spoonfuls into the tin, keeping colours evenly dispersed. After baking leave in the tin for 20 minutes then place onto a wire tray until cold.

RICH CHOCOLATE CAKE

Serves 16-20

BOURNEMOUTH

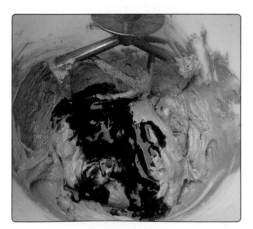

1. CAKE. *Beat together the butter and sugar. Thoroughly beat in the egg a little at a time. Stir in the treacle and essence.*

2. Sift together the flour, bicarbonate of soda, baking powder and salt. Fold into the creamed mixture.

3. Gradually fold in melted chocolate and sufficient milk to make into a thick batter. Divide mixture between tins and bake. Turn out onto a wire tray to cool.

4. FUDGE ICING. *Place all the ingredients into a heavy-based saucepan and heat gently, stirring until the sugar has melted.*

5. *Bring to the boil and cook to 116°C (240°F) or until the syrup, when dropped into cold water, will form a soft ball which can be squashed.*

INGREDIENTS

Metric		Imperial
145g	Butter	5oz
285g	Dark brown soft sugar	10oz
	3 eggs, size 3	
30ml	Black treacle	1oz
5ml	Vanilla essence	1tsp
225g	Plain flour	8oz
2.5ml	Bicarbonate of soda	½tsp
10ml	Baking powder	2tsp
	Pinch of salt	
225ml	Milk	8oz
57g	Cooking or plain chocolate, melted	2oz

FILLING

170g	Chocolate buttercream (see p5)	6oz

FUDGE ICING

455g	Caster sugar	1lb
150ml	Milk	¼pt
115g	Butter	4oz
30ml	Golden syrup	1oz
15ml	Cocoa powder	1tsp
57g	Cooking or plain chocolate	2oz

DECORATION

Chocolate curls
Cocoa powder

BAKING TIN

Two 21.5cm (8½in) round sandwich tin, greased.

BAKING

Preheated oven, 180°C or 360°F or gas mark 4
Middle shelf
30-35 minutes

Mary's Tips

Surprisingly little heat is required to soften chocolate. I recommend breaking the chocolate in a bowl over a saucepan of hot water, away from the heat source. Leave until melted. The smaller the chocolate blocks the easier (and faster) the process. Ensure no moisture enters the bowl. If you have a microwave, chocolate can easily be melted in it. Keep a close eye on progress to check the chocolate is not separated or even burnt.

6. *Remove from heat and leave to cool for 10 minutes, then beat until it is thick enough to spread.*

7. *Sandwich the sponges together with buttercream filling. Then quickly spread the fudge over the top and sides. Leave until set.*

8. *Decorate the cake-top with chocolate curls and then dust with cocoa powder.*

APPLE and WALNUT TEABREAD

Serves 8-10

1. *Sift together the flour, salt and mixed spice into a large bowl. Add all of the remaining ingredients.*

2. *Beat well together, using a spoon, to form an even blended mixture. Place mixture into the tin and level.*

3. *Sprinkle the top with a good layer of demerara sugar. After baking leave in the tin for 10 minutes then turn out onto a wire tray to cool.*

ARCADIA

INGREDIENTS

Metric		Imperial
225g	Self raising flour	8oz
	Pinch of salt	
5ml	Mixed spice	1tsp
115g	Soft tub margarine	4oz
115g	Caster sugar	4oz
	2 eggs, size 2	
15ml	Golden syrup	1tbsp
115g	Sultanas	4oz
57g	Walnuts, chopped	2oz
	1 medium cooking apple, peeled, cored and chopped.	

BAKING TIN

905g (2lb) loaf tin greased and base lined.

BAKING

Preheated oven, 180°C or 360°F or gas mark 4 for 1 hour then reduce heat to 170°C or 340°F or gas mark 3 for 20 minutes or until baked.

Mary's Tips

Teabread is often served with butter, but this one is so moist already that it is an unnecessary addition.

ORIENTAL CAKE

Serves 8-12

VINE HARVEST

EVESHAM GOLD

INGREDIENTS

Metric		Imperial
340g	Plain flour	12oz
	Pinch of salt	
170g	Butter or margarine	6oz
225g	Caster sugar	8oz
215ml	Milk	7½oz
	4 egg whites, size 2, beaten	
5ml	Cinnamon	1tsp
5ml	Grated nutmeg	1tsp
170g	Figs, finely chopped, ready to eat-no soak.	6oz
15ml	Golden syrup, warmed	1tbsp

BAKING TIN

21.5cm (8½in) round cake tin greased and fully lined with greaseproof paper.

BAKING

Preheated oven, 175°C or 350°F or gas mark 3½
Middle shelf
35-40 minutes

1. Sift the flour and salt together. Cream the butter and sugar, add the flour and the milk then fold in the beaten egg whites.

2. Divide the mixture in half; leave one half plain, and to the other add the spices, figs and syrup.

3. Place alternate spoonfuls of the two mixtures into the tin. After baking leave for 15 minutes then turn out onto a wire tray and dust with caster sugar.

1. *Melt the butter in a saucepan over gentle heat. Then remove from the heat. Whisk the eggs and sugar in a bowl over hot water until light and fluffy.*

2. *Remove the water and whisk until the mixture is cool. Sift the flours together and fold half into the mixture. Fold in half the melted butter.*

INGREDIENTS

Metric		Imperial
42g	Butter, melted	1½oz
	3 eggs, size 2	
85g	Caster sugar	3oz
71g	Plain flour	2½oz
15ml	Cornflour	1tbsp

FILLING

	Raspberry seedless jam	
285ml	Double cream, whipped	10oz
	Icing sugar for dusting	
	1 glacé cherry	

Two sponges are required, therefore double the mixture if your oven is large enough to take both tins for baking. If not make and bake one at a time.

BAKING TIN

21.5cm (8½in) round sandwich tin greased and base lined.

BAKING

Preheated oven, 180°C or 360°F or gas mark 4
Middle shelf
25-30 minutes

Mary's Tips

To make a light sponge, slightly warm the flour. If you allow the flour to be cold, it will chill the eggs which will release some of the air just beaten in. Remember, air is the only raising agent in a Genoese and you should do everything possible to incorporate and retain as much as possible.

Do not attempt to use granulated sugar as a substitute for caster sugar. It dissolves less easily and gives a speckly surface.

When cutting cold Genoese, I suggest twisting the knife from left to right. You may find a straight cut produces a ragged and crumbly edge.

3. *Gradually fold in remaining butter and flour alternately. Pour into tin and bake. After baking turn out onto a wire tray to cool. Cut out centre of one sponge.*

4. *Spread jam over the base sponge, place the ring on top. Fill the centre with the whipped cream to form a peak.*

5. *Cut the circle into required sections and place onto the cream. Then dust lightly with sifted icing sugar. Decorate with a glacé cherry.*

GENOESE SPONGE CAKE

Serves 16

RUM and CARAMEL LAYER

Serves 16-20

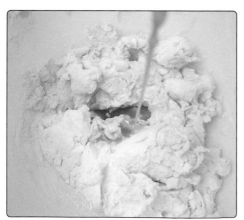

1. Beat the butter and sugar until light and fluffy. Gradually beat in the egg yolks. Sift dry ingredients together, fold in with alternate spoonfuls of the liquids.

2. Beat egg whites until stiff, gently fold into mixture. Divide mixture between the tins and bake. After baking, cool for 5 minutes then turn out onto a wire tray.

3. Beat all filling ingredients together until fluffy. Slice and sandwich the cakes together. Leave some filling for the sides. Brush top with boiling apricot purée.

INGREDIENTS

4. Place all ingredients for the toffee (except the vinegar) into a saucepan and heat gently. When boiling add the vinegar, stirring occasionally.

5. Boil for 10-15 minutes until caramel in colour. Then pour out onto a greased, non-stick tray and spread thinly. When cold break into small pieces.

Metric		Imperial
145g	Butter or margarine, softened	5oz
115g	Caster sugar	4oz
	2 eggs, size 2, separated	
225g	Plain flour	8oz
	Pinch of salt	
10ml	Baking powder	2tsp
115g	Orange juice	4oz
115ml	Rum	4oz

RUM CREAM FILLING

115g	Butter	4oz
340g	icing sugar, sifted	12oz
	2 egg whites, size 3, stiffly beaten	
	Rum flavouring	

TOFFEE FOR CAKE SIDES

225g	Caster sugar	8oz
28g	Butter	1oz
5ml	Golden syrup	1tsp
75ml	Water	⅛ pint
2.5ml	Vinegar	½tsp

GLACÉ ICING

225g	Icing sugar, sifted	8oz
	Few drops of flavouring	
	Approximately 45ml (3tbsp) water	
	Food colourings	

BAKING TINS

Two 18.5cm (7¼in) square tins greased and fully lined.

BAKING

Preheated oven, 180°C or 360°F or gas mark 4
Middle shelf
25 minutes

Mary's Tips

Though this recipe asks for rum flavouring in the cream filling, the real thing can certainly be used.

6. For the glacé icing, mix ingredients together, adjust water so that the consistency coats the back of a spoon. Colour a small amount for the lines.

7. Fill a piping bag with dark icing. Coat cake-top with main icing, then pipe lines one way and draw a cocktail stick across the other to form feathering.

8. When the icing has set, spread the sides with cream then cover with the toffee pieces.

INGREDIENTS
(for Rich Jamaican Loaf)

Metric		Imperial
85g	Margarine	3oz
115g	Light brown sugar	4oz
15ml	Golden syrup	1tbsp
15ml	Black treacle	1tbsp
	2 eggs, size 3, beaten	
225g	Mashed banana	8oz
225g	Self-raising flour	8oz
5ml	Mixed spice	1tsp
1.25ml	Bicarbonate of soda	¼tsp
1.25ml	Salt	¼tsp
225g	Raisins	8oz

FOR THE GLAZE

30ml	Warmed golden syrup	2tbsp

BAKING TIN

21.5 x 11.5cm (8½ x 4½in) loaf tin, greased and lined.

BAKING

Preheated oven at 180°C or 30°F or gas mark 4 for about 1½ hours.

INGREDIENTS
(for Yoghurt Loaf)

Metric		Imperial
115g	Plain flour	4oz
5ml	Baking powder	1tsp
2.5ml	Bicarbonate of soda	½tsp
2.5ml	Mixed spice	½tsp
2.5ml	Nutmeg	½tsp
2.5ml	Star Anise	½tsp
115g	Wholmeal flour	4oz
170g	Light brown sugar	6oz
	2 eggs, size 2	
75g	Sunflower oil	3oz
145g	Carton of black cherry yoghurt	6oz

BAKING TIN

21.5 x 11.5cm (8½ x 4½in) loaf tin, greased and lined.

BAKING

Preheated oven at 180°C or 30°F or gas mark 4 for about 1 hour.

RICH JAMAICAN LOAF

1. Cream the margarine and sugar together until light and fluffy. Stir in the treacle and syrup. Add the eggs and banana, and mix well.

2. Sieve the flour, spice, bicarbonate of soda and salt, and add to the creamed mixture with the raisins. Place in the greased and lined loaf tin.

3. Bake until well-risen and firm to the touch: about 1½ hours. Remove from tin, then glaze the top with melted golden syrup.

78

MARQUIS

YOGHURT LOAF

1. Sieve the plain flour, baking powder, bicarbonate of soda and spices. Add the wholemeal flour and the sugar.

2. Beat the eggs and add to the dry mixture with the oil and the yoghurt. Stir until smooth. Put into the prepared tin.

3. Bake for about 1 hour or until well-risen and golden in colour. Test with a skewer, it should come out clean. Cool on a wire tray.

BUTTER MADEIRA CAKE

Serves 10

Mary's Tips

Though this cake was traditionally eaten in the 19th century with a glass of Madeira wine in the morning, it is now widely regarded as a classic teatime cake.

INGREDIENTS

Metric		Imperial
170g	Butter	6oz
170g	Caster sugar	6oz
	3 eggs, size 3, beaten	
145g	Self-raising flour	5oz
115g	Plain flour	4oz
	Grated rind and juice of one orange	
28g	Crushed cube sugar	1oz
	Few strands of crystallised orange peel	

BAKING TIN

905g (2lb) loaf tin, greased

BAKING

Preheated oven at 170°C or 325°F or gas mark 3 for about 1 hour 15 minutes.

1. Beat together the butter and sugar until light. Beat in the eggs, one at a time. Fold in the flours.

2. Add the rind and juice of an orange, and stir well.

3. Put into the prepared tin, and smooth over. Sprinkle the crushed sugar and a few strands of crystallised orange peel over the top.

SULTANA and APPLE SCONE

Serves 8

1. Peel, core and finely chop the apple. Sift together flour, salt and baking powder. Rub in butter, then add sugar, apple and sultanas.

2. Mix to a soft, but not sticky dough with the beaten egg and a little milk.

3. Roll out on a floured table to 0.5cm (¼in) thick and about 20cm (8in) diameter. Make into 8 wedges and brush with a little milk and sugar before baking.

INGREDIENTS

Metric		Imperial
	1 medium cooking apple	
57g	Sultanas	2oz
225g	Self-raising flour, sifted	8oz
2.5ml	Salt	½tsp
5ml	Baking powder	1tsp
57g	Butter	2oz
57g	Caster sugar	2oz
	1 egg, size 3	
	Enough milk to mix to a soft dough	

FOR THE GLAZE

A little milk and caster sugar

BAKING TIN

21.5cm (8½in) round sandwich or flan tin lightly greased.

BAKING

Preheated oven at 200°C or 400°F or gas mark 6 for about 20 minutes.

Mary's Tips

Serve wedges of the scone while still warm, spread with butter.

QUICKIE SPONGE CAKES

1. Melt together the margarine, syrup and sugar over a gentle heat and then leave to cool a little.

2. Beat the egg into the milk and stir into the syrup mixture.

3. Sift flour into a bowl and beat in syrup mixture using a spoon, until smooth. Place into tin and bake. After baking turn out onto a wire tray until cold.

INGREDIENTS FOR BASIC MIXTURE

Metric		Imperial
57g	Margarine	**2oz**
115g	Golden syrup	**4oz**
57g	Caster sugar	**2oz**
	1 egg, size 2	
30ml	Milk	**2tbsp**
115g	Self raising flour	**4oz**

BAKING TIN

19cm (7½in) round sponge tin greased and base lined.

BAKING

Preheated oven, 190°C or 370°F or gas mark 5
Middle shelf
25 minutes

Mary's Tips

This cake has the appearance of
a sponge, though it is made by the melting method.
See below for when to add different flavour variations.

COFFEE
Add 10ml (2tsp) of instant coffee to the melted margarine and syrup mixture.

COCONUT
Add 50g (2oz) desicccated coconut to the flour after sifting.

CHOCOLATE
From the bowl of sieved flour, remove 15ml (1tbsp) and replace it with 15ml (1tbsp) cocoa powder.

ORANGE
Grate the rind of an orange finely and add to the raw mixture. Use the juice for glacé icing.

LEMON
As with orange, add the grated rind to the mixture, and use the lemon juice for glacé icing to cover the cake.

ALMOND
For a moist, rich cake, add 50g (2oz) of ground almonds to the flour after sifting.

GERMAN APPLE CAKE

Serves 10-12

1. BASE. Sift together flour, sugar and half ground almonds. Rub in the butter until mixture resembles fine crumbs. Mix in the egg and juice to form a dough.

INGREDIENTS

Metric		Imperial
170g	Self raising flour	6oz
85g	Light brown soft sugar	3oz
85g	Ground almonds	3oz
130g	Butter	4½oz
	1 egg, size 3, beaten	
7.5ml	Lemon juice	1½tsp
	FILLING	
680g	Cooking apples	1½lbs
130g	Light brown soft sugar	4½oz
7.5ml	Lemon juice	1½tsp
	TOPPING	
85g	Self raising flour	3oz
215g	Light brown soft sugar	7½oz
7.5ml	Powdered cinnamon	1½tsp
85g	Butter	3oz

BAKING TIN

21.5cm (8½in) round loose-bottomed cake tin greased and base lined.

BAKING

Preheated oven 180°C or 360°F or gas mark 4
Middle shelf
1-1½ hours
When baked leave in the tin until cold before removing. Then dust with icing sugar to serve.

2. Press dough evenly into the tin then cover with remaining ground almonds. FILLING. Peel and core apples, cut into slices, mix with sugar and lemon juice.

3. Place the prepared apples over base. TOPPING. Sift together the dry ingredients then mix in butter until crumbly. Sprinkle over apples and bake.

CRUNCHY HAZELNUT CAKE

Serves 16

EVESHAM GOLD AND NAPKIN

INGREDIENTS

Metric		Imperial
130g	Butter or margarine	4½oz
215g	Caster sugar	7½oz
	3 eggs, size 2	
170g	Ground hazelnuts	6oz
515g	Self raising flour, sifted with 1.25ml (¼tsp) salt	18oz
	Milk as required	

DECORATION

57g	Flaked hazelnuts	2oz

Mary's Tips

If flaked hazelnuts are difficult to find, buy whole ones and chop them roughly with a sharp knife on a steady board.

BAKING TIN

23cm (9in) ring tin, well greased.

BAKING

Preheated oven, 190°C or 370°F or gas mark 5 for 30 minutes then reduce heat to 160°C or 320°F or gas mark 2½ until baked. Middle shelf
Total cooking time 1-1¼ hours

1. Grease the ring tin and place the flaked hazelnuts evenly around the base. Cream the butter, add the sugar and beat until light and fluffy.

2. Beat in the eggs, one at a time. Mix in the ground hazelnuts. Fold in the sifted flour and salt, with sufficient milk to make a fairly soft consistency.

3. Spoon the mixture into the tin and bake. After baking leave in the tin for 30 minutes then turn out onto a wire tray to cool.

STRAWBERRY and ALMOND CAKE

Serves 16

MARQUIS

1. Whisk the eggs and sugar together in a bowl over a pan of hot water, until the mixture is light and thick and holds the shape of a figure 8.

2. Lightly fold in the sieved flour, then blend in the melted butter and essence with the last of the flour.

3. Immediately pour into the tin and bake. After baking turn out onto a wire tray until cold. Then slice into three layers.

4. FILLING. Beat together the butter and sugar until light and fluffy. Beat in the ground almonds.

INGREDIENTS

Metric		Imperial
	CAKE	
	3 eggs, size 3	
85g	Caster sugar	3oz
85g	Plain flour, sifted	3oz
28g	Butter, melted	1oz
	Almond essence	
	FILLING	
225g	Fresh strawberries	8oz
115g	Butter	4oz
85g	Caster sugar	3oz
85g	Ground almonds	3oz
145ml	Thick cream	5oz
90ml	Amaretto liqueur	6tbsp
	TOPPING	
145ml	Thick cream	5oz
	Toasted flaked almonds	

BAKING TIN

905g (2lb) loaf tin greased and fully lined.

BAKING

Preheated oven, 180°C or 360°F or gas mark 4
Middle shelf
25 minutes

5. Beat in cream a little at a time to avoid curdling, then beat in the liqueur. Re-line the tin with greaseproof paper, then grease the paper lightly with butter.

Mary's Tips

Any other soft fruit can be used for this cake, particularly fresh raspberries, peaches, nectarines or blackberries.

It is important to allow the cake time to cool on a wire tray. Trapped steam will be retained in the cake if it is left in its tin and this will make the cake heavy. Conversely, most fruit and wedding cakes textures are improved by being kept in the tin.

6. Place the small layer of sponge into the tin and sprinkle with liqueur, then place in strawberries cut in half.

7. Cover with half the filling, then repeat step 6 and 7. Place the last slice of sponge on top, sprinkle with liqueur and chill overnight.

8. Turn out onto the serving plate. Decorate with whipped cream, strawberries and flaked almonds.

THE MARY FORD STORY

Michael and Mary Ford have prepared and photographed all of the cakes and recipes in this book. The story of how they came to publish their own "step-by-step" books stretches back to the 1970's.

In the 1970's in Bournemouth, England - Michael and Mary Ford provided tuition classes in the arts of cake decoration and confectionery. The business grew steadily and developed into related areas. From tuition classes a mail order service was started to serve students once they had completed their courses.

From the early days of the classes Mary Ford felt there was a great demand for a "step-by-step" illustrated instruction course. A set of cake designs was produced in loose leaf form and extensively used in the classes and through the mail order service. Encouraged by the success of these, a decision was taken to produce a full colour hardback book.

The decision to produce such a book coincided with Mary Ford receiving much publicity from her preparing and decorating an immaculate wedding cake for the marriage of HRH the Prince of Wales and Lady Diana Spencer. Financial support for the costs of preparing a book was provided in part from the advanced orders placed by the loyal members of the mail order list.

During 1982, Mary started decorating and Michael started photographing the "step-by-step" stages and the finished cakes and just

before Christmas 1982 the first 12,500 copies of "101 Cake Designs" were delivered and despatched. Since then the book has been reprinted many times and has now sold over 200,000 copies worldwide. It has been described as the "Bible" of cake decoration and as "the next best thing to having Mary standing alongside you in the kitchen".

Included in all the 1982 and 1983 editions of "101 Cake Designs" was a questionnaire asking readers if they would like a follow-up title and suggesting a number of possible subjects (Cake Decoration, Confectionery, Bread Making etc.). The response to the questionnaire was exceptional and strongly in favour of a second cake decoration title. Accordingly, Mary returned to her turntable and Michael to his camera and "Another 101 Cake Designs" was launched in 1984.

Whilst Michael and Mary Ford continued with the tuition, bakery and equipment side until 1991, it became apparent that the demand for the step-by-step books was such that they needed to dedicate their time exclusively to this area.

The Mary Ford books have now sold over 800,000 copies around the world and she is a leading name in cake decoration. Her books have brought pleasure and guidance to the most inexperienced beginner in preparing a birthday cake and to the professional decorator in completing the most intricate sugarflower.

Mary Ford operates a mail order service for her books. Details can be found on page 190.

MARY FORD
BISCUIT RECIPES

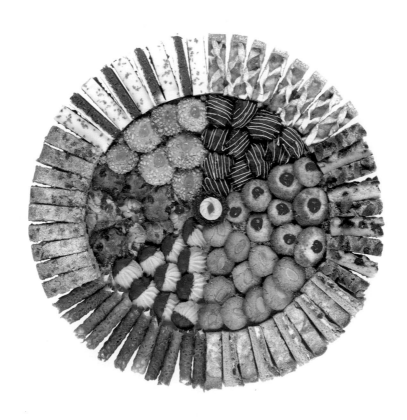

SUGAR

Sugar, an essential ingredient in the kitchen, originates in the giant grass-like sugar cane which grows in tropical climates such as the Caribbean, Mauritius and Fiji. It is a flavour enhancer, preservative and natural sweetener as well as contributing to the texture of food.

Sugar can aptly be described as 'a taste of sunshine' because it is manufactured in plants as a direct result of the sun's energy, through a process known as photosynthesis. However, whilst all plants make sugars, commercially produced sugars are extracted only from sugar cane and sugar beet.
The extraction process used by Tate & Lyle removes undesirable impurities and produces the characteristic crystalline structure without the addition of any artificial colourings, flavourings or preservatives.

Nutritionally brown and white sugars are virtually identical, but the distinctive colour and flavour of brown sugar arises from molasses, which is the syrup remaining after all the sugar has been removed from the cane juice. When manufacturing white sugar, the molasses is completely removed whilst the different brown sugars contain more, or less, of the syrup depending on the flavour and colour required.
Therefore, careful selection of the type of sugar used can greatly enhance the finished taste and texture.

Icing Sugar: The finest of all sugars. It dissolves rapidly and is especially used in making icings, smooth toppings, confectionery, meringues and cake frostings. Apart from decorating cakes, icing sugar is perfect for sweetening cold drinks and uncooked desserts, as its fine texture makes it easy to dissolve.

Granulated Sugar: Granulated sugar has a very pure crystal and is an ideal boiling sugar. It can be used for sweetening tea, coffee, sprinkling over cereals or frosting cakes and glasses for decoration.

Caster Sugar: Caster sugar is a free flowing sugar with very fine crystals. Excellent for use in baking cakes and other baked goods as the fine white grains ensure smooth blending and an even texture.

Lyle's Golden Syrup: Golden syrup is a partially inverted syrup produced from intermediate refinery sugar liquors when they are heated in the presence of an acid. It is an ideal sweetener and can be used in cooking and baking to add bulk, texture and taste.

Lyle's Black Treacle: Black treacle is a dark, viscous liquid with a characteristic flavour. It is obtained from cane molasses, a by product of sugar refining.

Demerara Sugar: This sugar has a golden colour with a unique flavour that makes it particularly popular in coffee. The grain is larger than granulated and is ideal for decorating biscuits and cakes, sprinkling over desserts and making crunchy toppings.

Light Brown Soft Sugar: This sugar is fine grained, creamy golden in colour and has a mild syrup flavour. It is best used when creamed with butter or margarine in any recipe that requires a deeper, richer colour and fuller flavour.

Dark Brown Soft Sugar: This sugar is darker with a strong flavour and is ideal for rich fruit cakes, gingerbread, spiced teabreads and puddings.

CURRY TWISTS

INGREDIENTS
Makes 48

Metric		Imperial
85g	Wholemeal self-raising flour	3oz
85g	Self-raising flour, sifted	3oz
	Pinch of salt	
5ml	Curry powder	1tsp
115g	Margarine	4oz
5ml	Dark brown soft sugar	1tsp
15ml	Sesame seeds	1tbsp
	1 egg yolk	
15-30ml	Milk	1-2tbsp

TOPPING

	Milk to glaze	
15-30ml	Sesame seeds	1-2tbsp

BAKING TRAYS

Well greased baking trays.

BAKING

Preheated oven, 190°C, 375°F
or gas mark 5
Middle shelf
15 minutes or until golden brown

1. Place wholemeal flour, white flour, salt and curry powder in a bowl. Rub in the margarine until mixture resembles breadcrumbs. Stir in the brown sugar and sesame seeds.

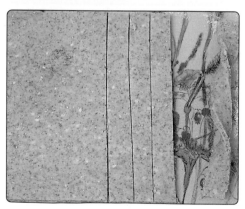

2. Mix in the egg yolk and sufficient milk to make a fairly soft, pliable dough. Roll out on lightly floured surface and cut narrow strips and carefully twist one at a time.

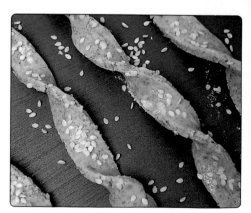

3. Place onto the tray and brush with milk then sprinkle with sesame seeds and bake. Leave on the trays to cool slightly before placing onto wire trays.

JAM BANDITS

INGREDIENTS

Makes 12

Metric		Imperial
225g	Plain flour	8oz
5ml	Baking powder	1tsp
10ml	Ground cinnamon	2tsp
115g	Butter	4oz
85g	Lyle's golden syrup	3oz
	1 egg yolk	

FILLING

Jam or preserve of choice

DECORATION

Icing sugar for dusting

BAKING TIN

Well greased 20.5cm (8in) square, shallow baking tin.

BAKING

Preheated oven, 190°C, 375°F
or gas mark 5
Middle shelf
30 minutes

Mary's Tips

Rinse measures and spoons
in hot water before use,
then syrup can be scraped
off cleanly without waste.

1. *Sift together the flour, baking powder and cinnamon. Rub in the butter until breadcrumb texture is formed.*

2. *Mix in the syrup and yolk to form a smooth dough. Divide the dough in half and then roll out and fit one portion evenly into the tin.*

3. *Spread a generous amount of filling onto the base then cover with the remaining dough and bake. After baking leave to cool before cutting into fingers.*

CHEQUERS

1. Beat the butter until soft and creamy, then beat in the sugar until light and fluffy.

2. Sift the flour into the creamed mixture and rub together to form a crumble texture. Divide the mixture into two equal portions then mix the drinking chocolate into one portion.

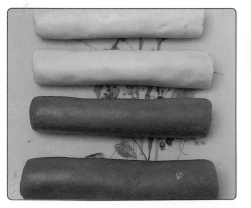

3. Continue mixing until crumbs bind together. Divide each portion into two and roll out to 20.5cm (8in) long. Wrap in foil and chill until firm.

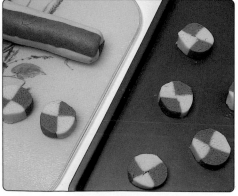

4. When chilled cut each roll into four. Join alternate colours together using a little water. Cut into slices, place onto trays and bake.

INGREDIENTS
Makes 36

Metric		Imperial
145g	Butter or margarine	**5oz**
115g	Caster sugar	**4oz**
255g	Plain flour	**9oz**
7.5ml	Drinking chocolate	**1½tsp**

BAKING TRAYS

Well greased baking trays.

BAKING

Preheated oven, 180°C, 360°F
or gas mark 4
Middle shelf
8-10 minutes or until just firm

BROWNIES

INGREDIENTS
Makes 24

Metric		Imperial
115g	Butter or margarine	4oz
115g	Plain Scotbloc or Chocolat	4oz
115g	Dark brown soft sugar	4oz
115g	Self-raising flour	4oz
	Pinch of salt	
	2 eggs, size 3	
60g	Walnuts, chopped	2oz
15-30ml	Milk	1-2tbsp

TOPPING

115g	Milk or plain Scotbloc or Chocolat	4oz
60g	Unsalted butter	2oz
	1 egg, size 3	
170g	Icing sugar, sifted	6oz

BAKING TIN

Greased and lined with greaseproof paper 18 x 28cm (7 x 11in) shallow baking tin.

BAKING

Preheated oven, 180°C, 360°F or gas mark 4
Middle shelf
30-40 minutes

Mary's Tips

A soft dropping consistency is when the mixture just drops off the spoon.

If using a fan oven, the baking temperature may need adjusting.

This rich, moist traybake will store very well uncut in an airtight tin.

If you are watching the calories, this traybake is equally good without the topping.

1. Place the butter and chocolate together in a bowl over a saucepan of hot water and leave until melted. Remove from the heat and stir in the sugar. Leave to cool.

2. Sift the flour with the salt into a mixing bowl. Make a well in the centre and pour in the cooled chocolate mixture. Mix together well.

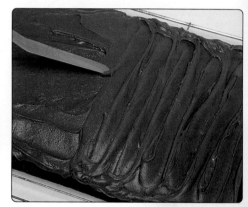

3. Beat in the eggs and walnuts. Stir in sufficient milk to give a soft dropping consistency. Spread the mixture evenly in the tin and bake. Leave to cool in the tin.

4. For the topping, melt the chocolate and butter in a pan over hot water, stirring occasionally.

5. Thoroughly beat the egg and stir into the chocolate. Remove from the heat and stir in the icing sugar. Then beat well.

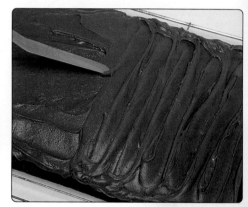

6. Leave to cool slightly until the mixture thickens. Place the base onto a wire tray then spread the mixture with a palette knife over the top. Cut into squares.

MELTING CHOCOLATE

This method should be used to melt chocolate flavoured coatings such as Scotbloc or Chocolat.

Melt the chocolate slowly on a very low heat, stirring gently. Stand the bowl over a saucepan which is small enough to support it without the bowl touching the base. The water level should not be allowed to touch the bowl and the water should simmer, not boil. Never try to hurry the melting process by turning up the heat. When the chocolate is almost melted, remove from the heat and continue stirring until the chocolate is smooth and completely

melted. Keep it warm, stirring occasionally, to prevent it from setting while in use.

To melt Scotbloc in a microwave:

Place 225g (8oz) of broken plain Scotbloc in a non-metallic bowl. Microwave for 4-5 minutes on a medium setting, stirring once. When just softened, remove from the microwave and stir well until the chocolate has completely melted. It is important not to overheat beyond the point where the chocolate is just soft, as this makes it grainy and unmanageable. Milk Scotbloc will need slightly less time.

WHISKY SNAPS

1. Melt the syrup, sugar and butter together gently in a saucepan. Stir in the whisky. Sift the flour and ground ginger together.

2. Mix all the ingredients together until well blended. Drop teaspoonfuls onto the trays about 15cm (6in) apart and bake.

INGREDIENTS

Makes 36

Metric		Imperial
115g	Lyle's golden syrup	4oz
115g	Light brown soft sugar	4oz
115g	Butter	4oz
5ml	Whisky	1tsp
115g	Plain flour	4oz
10ml	Ground ginger	2tsp

FILLING

285g	Whipping cream	10oz

BAKING TRAYS

Well greased baking trays.

BAKING

Preheated oven, 180°C, 360°F or gas mark 4
Middle shelf
Approximately 10 minutes or until golden brown

Mary's Tips

Roll the snaps around the handles as soon as possible before they harden. If too cool then return to oven to soften.

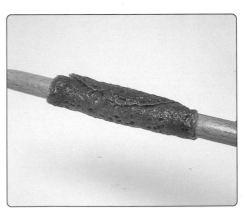

3. Immediately after baking leave to cool for a few seconds before rolling round the greased handle of a large wooden spoon. Slide off and fill with whipped cream when cold.

STICKLEBACKS

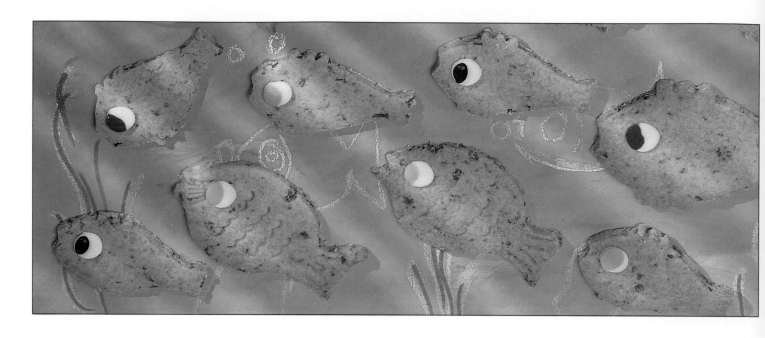

INGREDIENTS

Metric		Imperial
85g	Plain flour	3oz
85g	Self-raising flour	3oz
115g	Butter	4oz
60g	Light brown soft sugar	2oz
30g	Bran flakes, crushed finely	1oz

DECORATION

A little piece of sugarpaste or royal icing for the fish eyes

BAKING TRAYS

Well greased baking trays.

BAKING

Preheated oven, 180°C, 360°F
or gas mark 4
Middle shelf
Approximately 20 minutes or until golden brown

Mary's Tips

Place equal sized fish on each tray to keep even colour when baking.

1. *Sift the flours into a bowl then rub in the butter and sugar to give a breadcrumb mixture. Then add in the bran flakes.*

2. *Knead together to form a smooth, well mixed dough.*

3. *Roll the mixture on a lightly floured surface, cut out the fish and place onto trays and bake.*

PEANUT CHEWS

INGREDIENTS
Makes 36

Metric		Imperial
115g	Butter	4oz
85g	Low fat soft cheese	3oz
2.5ml	Vanilla essence	½tsp
170g	Caster sugar	6oz
225g	Plain flour	8oz
	Pinch of salt	
115g	Peanuts, finely chopped	4oz

BAKING TRAYS

Well greased baking trays.

BAKING

Preheated oven, 190°C, 375°F
or gas mark 5
Middle shelf
Approximately 12 minutes or until
golden brown around the edges

Mary's Tips

Walnuts, finely chopped, can be substituted for peanuts.
This will give a stronger flavour.

1. Blend the butter, soft cheese and essence together. Gradually beat in the sugar until light and creamy.

2. Sift the flour and salt together into the mixture, add the chopped peanuts and blend to a soft dough.

3. Mould the dough into a roll and cut into 36 pieces. Mould into rounds, place onto trays and flatten slightly before marking with a fork. After baking leave on wire tray to cool.

LEMON FINGERS

1. *Place all the ingredients in a mixing bowl and beat for three minutes on medium speed or for 5 minutes by hand with a wooden spoon.*

2. *Spread the mixture evenly into the prepared tin and bake. After baking place on a wire tray, remove the paper and leave until cold.*

3. *Mix the topping ingredients together to form a smooth, not too soft, icing. Spread over the sponge and leave to set before cutting. Decorate as required.*

INGREDIENTS
Makes 30

Metric		Imperial
145g	Soft tub margarine	5oz
145g	Caster sugar	5oz
	Grated rind of 1 lemon	
	3 eggs, size 3	
145g	Self-raising flour	5oz
200g	Icing sugar, sifted	7oz
30ml	Lemon juice	2tbsp
	A little water	
	A few drops of yellow colouring	

DECORATION

Lemons made from sugarpaste or lemon slices

BAKING TIN

Greased and lined with greaseproof paper18 x 28cm (7 x 11in) shallow baking tin.

BAKING

Preheated oven, 180°C, 360°F or gas mark 4
Middle shelf
30-35 minutes

Mary's Tips

The grated rind and juice of orange or lime can be used to vary the flavour.

Decorate with sugarpaste, limes or oranges.

GINGERBREAD BISCUITS

Increase the size of templates to that required.

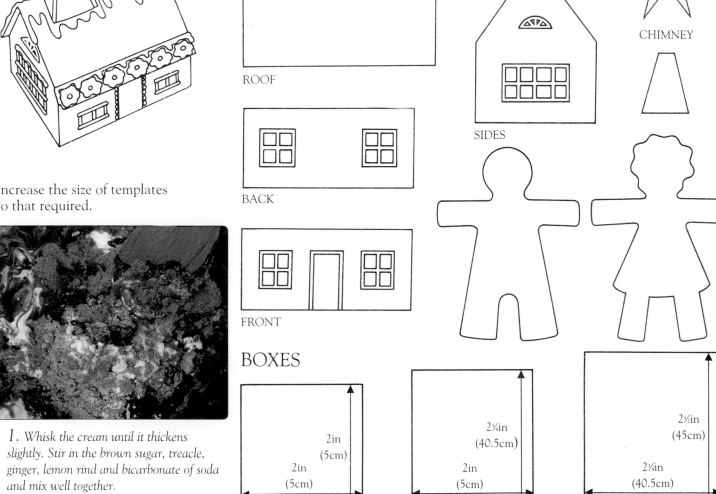

ROOF

BACK

FRONT

SIDES

CHIMNEY

BOXES

2in
(5cm)

2in
(5cm)

2¼in
(40.5cm)

2in
(5cm)

2½in
(45cm)

2¼in
(40.5cm)

1. Whisk the cream until it thickens slightly. Stir in the brown sugar, treacle, ginger, lemon rind and bicarbonate of soda and mix well together.

2. Immediately sift the flour into the mixture and gradually stir in.

3. Continue working in the flour until a smooth, pliable dough is formed. Roll out on lightly floured surface and cut the pieces required using the templates as a guide.

4. Carefully place onto the trays, without distorting the shapes then brush with water and bake. Remove from the trays to cool. Then fix boxes and decorate with royal icing.

INGREDIENTS

Metric		Imperial
170ml	Double cream	6floz
225g	Light brown soft sugar	8oz
225g	Lyle's black treacle	8oz
10ml	Ground ginger	2tsp
	Grated rind of 1 lemon	
10ml	Bicarbonate of soda	2tsp
570g	Plain flour	20oz

DECORATION

Royal icing
Variety of sweets

BAKING TRAYS

Well greased baking trays.

BAKING

Approximately 20-25 minutes, depending on thickness of biscuit

Preheated oven, 180°C, 360°F or gas mark 4
Middle shelf

Mary's Tips

This recipe is ideal for any cut-out shapes. Use the templates for a Gingerbread house to make an attractive centrepiece for a Christmas party.

To make the boxes, use the templates to cut out base and sides. Use a contrasting colour royal icing to secure pieces and then overpipe edges to neaten.

The eyes on the figure can be indented before baking.

Use Tate & Lyle traditional royal icing for quickness.

ALMOND MACAROONS

1. Mix the caster sugar, ground almonds and rice flour together in a bowl. Lightly whisk the egg whites.

2. Add sufficient beaten egg whites to the dry ingredients to form a stiff dough. Mould the dough to a long roll and cut into 16 pieces. Mould each piece into a ball.

INGREDIENTS

Makes 16

Metric		Imperial
170g	Caster sugar	6oz
115g	Ground almonds	4oz
5ml	Rice flour	1tsp
	1-2 egg whites	

DECORATION

Caster sugar for sprinkling
Split almonds

BAKING TRAYS

Well greased baking trays.

BAKING

Preheated oven, 180°C, 360°F
or gas mark 4
Middle shelf
Approximately 15 minutes or until
light brown

Mary's Tips

For variety: Omit the almonds and dip half the biscuit into melted chocolate when cool.

Always use eggs at room temperature for baking.

3. Place onto trays, allowing plenty of room for spreading during baking. Brush with remaining egg white, add a split almond then sprinkle with a little caster sugar and bake.

BANANA BREAKFAST SNACKS

Mary's Tips

These snacks freeze well.

Wrap in foil or place in a plastic container.

Will keep for up to two months.

1. Sift the flour and baking powder together into a mixing bowl. Stir in the muesli and sunflower seeds.

INGREDIENTS
Makes 16

Metric		Imperial
225g	Wholemeal self-raising flour	8oz
10ml	Baking powder	2tsp
145g	Unsweetened muesli	5oz
45g	Sunflower seeds	1½oz
170g	Butter	6oz
170g	Light brown soft sugar	6oz
	4 bananas	
	Juice of 1 lemon	
15ml	Sesame seeds	1tbsp

BAKING TIN

Lightly greased and lined with greaseproof paper 18 x 28cm (7 x 11in) shallow baking tin.

BAKING

Preheated oven, 180°C, 360°F or gas mark 4
Middle shelf
Approximately 40 minutes

2. Gently melt the butter in a saucepan then add the sugar and heat for a further 1-2 minutes. Mix thoroughly into the dry ingredients.

3. Spread two thirds into the prepared tin evenly. Peel and slice the bananas and toss in lemon juice then scatter into the tin.

4. Spoon the remaining mixture on top. Evenly sprinkle with sesame seeds and bake. Leave to cool in the tin then cut into squares.

SAVOURY WHIRLS

INGREDIENTS

Makes 15-20

Metric		Imperial
115g	Margarine	4oz
5ml	Light brown soft sugar	1tsp
145g	Plain flour	5oz
	Large pinch each of salt, pepper and paprika	
15ml	Sesame seeds	1tbsp
30ml	Parmesan cheese, grated	2tbsp
	Little milk (optional)	

DECORATION

Parmesan cheese, grated
Walnut pieces

BAKING TRAYS

Well greased baking trays.

BAKING

Preheated oven, 190°C, 375°F
or gas mark 5
Middle shelf
Approximately 15 minutes

1. Cream the margarine and sugar until soft. Sift the flour, salt, pepper and paprika together then mix in the sesame seeds and grated cheese.

2. Gradually work the dry ingredients into the creamed margarine to form a medium, soft dough. Mix in a few drops of milk if too stiff.

3. Fill a savoy bag, and star tube, with the mixture and pipe rosettes onto the prepared tins. Sprinkle with grated cheese then place walnut pieces on top and bake.

117

1. Melt the syrup, sugar, butter and water in a bowl over low heat. Leave until cool.

2. Mix in the egg yolk and grated rind. Sift the cocoa powder and spices together with 170g (6oz) of the flour and beat into the mixture.

3. Thoroughly beat in the chopped almonds, peel and raisins.

4. Sift the remaining flour together with the baking powder and fold into the mixture. Gently knead on floured surface until well blended. Roll out to 6mm (¼in) thick.

5. Cut into rounds and bake. Beat the topping ingredients together to form a coating consistency. When biscuits are cold cover with the topping and decorate with piping.

Mary's Tips

It is important to thoroughly sift the dry ingredients three times.

A coating consistency runs off the spoon easily.

Cover the biscuits with water icing or for a more professional finish, use royal icing. Royal icing should always be used for piping.

WATER ICING

Metric		Imperial
15ml	Boiling water	1tbsp
60ml	Icing sugar, sifted	4tbsp
	Colour and flavouring to taste	

Place water into a bowl. Gradually stir in enough icing sugar to make a smooth paste which will coat and slowly drop off the back of a spoon.

ROYAL ICING

Metric		Imperial
115g	Icing sugar	4oz
	1 egg white, lightly beaten	
	Few drops of lemon juice	
	Choice of food colours	

Sift icing sugar into a bowl. Beat in egg white and continue beating until soft peak consistency. Add a few drops of glycerine for a softer eating icing.

GIGI'S CINNAMON STARS

INGREDIENTS

Makes 30

Metric		Imperial
	3 egg whites, size 3	
255g	Caster sugar	9oz
315g	Ground almonds	11oz
15ml	Ground cinnamon	1tbsp
	Icing sugar for dusting	

BAKING TRAYS

Bake on trays lined with parchment or rice paper.

BAKING

Preheated oven, 160°C, 320°F or gas mark 3
Middle shelf
20-25 minutes or until the meringue topping is golden brown

Mary's Tips

When making meringue, always sterilise the bowl and whisk with boiling water before use.

1. Whisk the egg whites until stiff and then fold in the caster sugar with a large spoon. Set aside 60ml (4tbsp) of the mixture for the topping.

2. Fold the ground almonds and cinnamon into the remaining mixture to form a dough.

3. Using icing sugar for dusting, roll out to 1cm (½in) thick then cut into star shapes and place onto prepared trays.

4. Spread a little of the meringue topping over each biscuit then bake until light golden brown.

DINOSAURUS

1. Mix together the butter, sugar, baking powder, juice and essence until light and fluffy.

2. Gradually stir in the flour until well mixed then knead to form a soft dough. Place in refrigerator for 2-3 hours until firm enough to roll out.

INGREDIENTS

Metric		Imperial
225g	Butter	8oz
170g	Caster sugar	6oz
	1 egg, size 3	
5ml	Baking powder	1tsp
30ml	Orange juice	2tbsp
5ml	Vanilla essence	1tsp
285g	Plain flour, sifted	10oz

DECORATION

Water icing (see page 27)
Plain or milk Scotbloc or Chocolat

BAKING TRAYS

Well greased baking trays.

BAKING

Preheated oven, 200°C, 400°F
or gas mark 6
Middle shelf
6-10 minutes or until edges are
lightly browned

Mary's Tips

Any shape cutter can be used.

These biscuits colour very quickly
so careful baking is essential.

3. Roll out the dough and cut around card shapes or with cutters. Place onto the trays and bake. Decorate with water icing and melted chocolate (see page 15).

MINCEMEAT SHORTBREAD

1. Cream the fat and sugar then gradually work in the sifted flour and mincemeat. Knead the mixture until well blended.

2. Roll out on a lightly floured surface then press evenly into the tin. Mark around the edge with a fork.

3. Press with a spoon to form pattern shown. Cut into 8 sections then prick all over and bake. After baking cut again, sprinkle with caster sugar then leave until cold.

INGREDIENTS
Makes 8

Metric		Imperial
115g	Margarine or butter	4oz
60g	Caster sugar	2oz
170g	Plain flour, sifted	6oz
60ml	Mincemeat	4tbsp

DECORATION

A little caster sugar

BAKING TIN

21.5cm (8½in) round sponge tin greased with margarine or butter.

BAKING

Preheated oven, 170°C, 340°F or gas mark 3
Middle shelf
25-30 minutes or until golden brown.

Mary's Tips

This is an excellent way of using up leftover mincemeat from Christmas.
Makes 8 or more pieces.

HAZELNUT COOKIES

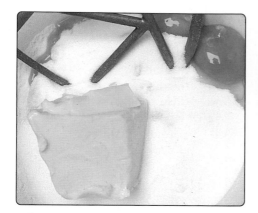

1. Place all the ingredients into a bowl and, using a beater on slow speed, blend together.

2. Remove from the bowl and gently knead together to form a smooth, firm dough. Leave to chill in the refrigerator for 1 hour.

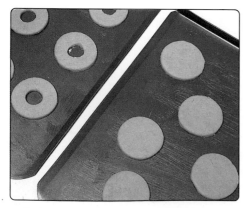

3. Roll out and cut into whole rounds and rings and then bake. When cold fix together with jam or preserve, dust with icing sugar and fill tops with piping jelly.

INGREDIENTS
Makes 30

Metric		Imperial
145g	Plain flour, sifted	5oz
145g	Butter	5oz
145g	Caster sugar	5oz
145g	Ground hazelnuts	5oz
	2 egg yolks	

DECORATION

Icing sugar for dusting
Jam or preserve
Piping jelly

BAKING TRAYS

Well greased baking trays.

BAKING

Preheated oven, 180°C, 360°F
or gas mark 4
Middle shelf
Approximately 15 minutes or until
golden brown

Mary's Tips

Piping jelly is available from most supermarkets.

Ensure ingredients are at room temperature before mixing.

NUT MERINGUE SLICES

INGREDIENTS
Makes 16

Metric		Imperial
60g	Light brown soft sugar	2oz
85g	Margarine	3oz
	2 egg yolks	
170g	Self-raising flour	6oz
5ml	Vanilla essence	1tsp

TOPPING

	2 egg whites	
85g	Caster sugar	3oz
30g	Walnuts, chopped	1oz
30g	Glacé cherries, chopped	1oz

BAKING TIN

Well greased 18 x 28cm (7 x 11in) shallow baking tin.

BAKING

Preheated oven, 180°C, 360°F or gas mark 4
Middle shelf
20-25 minutes

Mary's Tips

For a good meringue always whisk the egg whites first until very stiff before adding the sugar. Use a sterilised, grease free bowl and whisk. Never use a wooden spoon for meringue.

Separating the eggs overnight helps the meringue to whisk stiffly.

1. Cream the brown sugar and margarine together. Gradually beat in the egg yolks.

2. Sift the flour and stir into the creamed mixture together with the essence to form pastry.

3. Roll the pastry on a lightly floured surface and gently press into the base of the tin.

4. Whisk the egg whites until stiff then add half the caster sugar. Whisk until very stiff.

5. Fold in the remaining sugar, chopped walnuts and cherries until evenly blended.

6. Spread the mixture over the pastry base to within 1cm (½in) of the edges and then bake. Cut into bars whilst still warm then leave in the tin until cold.

NO COOK TREATS

INGREDIENTS
Makes 28

Metric		Imperial
285g	Lyle's golden syrup	10oz
225g	Peanut butter	8oz
5ml	Vanilla essence	1tsp
225g	Cereal Bran	8oz
60g	Chopped peanuts	2oz

TOPPING

115g	Plain or milk Scotbloc or Chocolat	4oz

BAKING TIN

Well greased 18 x 28cm (7 x 11in) shallow baking tin.

1. Mix the syrup and peanut butter together in a large saucepan and cook over medium heat stirring until mixture begins to boil.

2. Remove from the heat and stir in the essence, bran cereal and chopped peanuts until well blended.

3. Spread the mixture into the prepared tin and lightly press out evenly. Chill for 1 hour.

4. Turn out onto greaseproof paper. Melt the chocolate (see page 15) and spread over the top using a palette knife or serrated scraper. Cut into squares when set.

ALMOND SHORTBREAD

1. *Beat the butter until light and fluffy then thoroughly beat in the sugar.*

2. *Lightly fold in the flour, ground rice together with the nibbed or chopped almonds. Gently roll the mixture on a lightly floured surface.*

3. *Cut out circles, then place on trays. Press a flaked almond on top and bake. After baking sprinkle with caster sugar then leave to cool.*

INGREDIENTS
Makes 24

Metric		Imperial
115g	Butter	4oz
60g	Caster sugar	2oz
115g	Plain flour, sifted	4oz
60g	Ground rice	2oz
30g	Nibbed or chopped almonds	1oz

DECORATION

Caster sugar
Flaked almonds

BAKING TRAY

Lightly greased baking trays.

BAKING

Preheated oven 190°C, 375°F
or gas mark 5
Middle shelf
10-15 minutes or until light brown

AUSTRIAN STREUSELS

1. *For the sponge cake combine the margarine, sugar, egg, milk and flour using a beater on slow speed.*

2. *For the filling mix the ingredients in a bowl to form a crumbly texture. Spread half the cake mixture into the tin then sprinkle half the filling on top.*

INGREDIENTS
Makes 16

Metric		Imperial
85g	Soft tub margarine	3oz
170g	Caster sugar	6oz
	1 egg, size 3	
100ml	Milk	3½fl oz
170g	Self-raising flour, sifted	6oz

FILLING

85g	Light brown soft sugar	3oz
30g	Self-raising flour, sifted	1oz
5ml	Cinnamon	1tsp
30g	Soft margarine, melted	1oz
60g	Walnuts, chopped	2oz

BAKING TIN

Well greased 20.5cm (8in) square baking tin.

BAKING

Preheated oven, 170°C, 340°F or gas mark 3
Middle shelf
35-40 minutes

Mary's Tips

Serve warm or cold with coffee.

3. *Spread remaining cake mixture on top then cover with the remaining filling and bake. Cut into squares when cold.*

APPLE and DATE SHORTCAKE

1. Beat the fat and sugar until light and fluffy. Gradually beat in the egg a little at a time.

2. Sift the flour then stir into the mixture to form a well blended pastry. Roll out and place half the mixture into the tin.

3. Mix the apples and dates together and spread onto the pastry. Place remaining pastry on top and bake. When baked sprinkle with caster sugar and cut into bars when cold.

INGREDIENTS
Makes 12-16

Metric		Imperial
115g	Butter or margarine	4oz
85g	Caster sugar	3oz
	1 egg, size 3	
170g	Self-raising flour	6oz
225g	Cooking apples, cooked	8oz
115g	Dates, chopped	4oz

BAKING TIN

Lightly greased 18cm (7in) square shallow tin.

BAKING

Preheated oven, 180°C, 360°F or gas mark 4
Middle shelf
35-40 minutes

DECORATION

A little caster sugar for dusting

144

CHOCOLATE WALNUT BARS

Mary's Tips

For variation, try Lyle's black treacle as a substitute for golden syrup in the topping.

Then sprinkle with coconut.

INGREDIENTS
Makes 16

Metric		Imperial
85g	Margarine	3oz
115g	Plain flour	4oz
85g	Rolled oats	3oz
2.5ml	Baking powder	½tsp
115g	Demerara sugar	4oz

TOPPING

Metric		Imperial
85g	Plain Scotbloc or Chocolat	3oz
85g	Milk Scotbloc or Chocolat	3oz
60g	Margarine	2oz
225g	Lyle's golden syrup	8oz
60g	Plain flour	2oz
5ml	Vanilla essence	1tsp
115g	Walnuts, chopped	4oz

DECORATION

60g	White Scotbloc, melted	2oz

BAKING TIN

Well greased 18 x 28cm (7 x 11in) shallow baking tin.

BAKING

Preheated oven, 180°C, 360°F or gas mark 4
Middle shelf
After 10 minutes add the topping then bake for a further 20-25 minutes

1. For the base, melt the margarine, remove from heat and stir in the flour, oats, baking powder and sugar. Mix well then spread evenly in the tin and bake for 10 minutes.

2. For the topping, melt the chocolate with the margarine and syrup. Remove from heat and stir in the flour, essence and walnuts.

3. After the base has been baking for 10 minutes, remove from oven and spread the topping mixture evenly over the base and return to the oven for 20-25 minutes.

4. Cool in the tin for 10 minutes, then loosen around the edges and cut into bars.

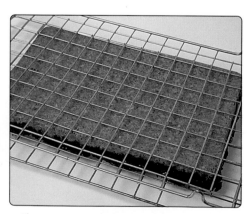

5. Place a wire tray over the tin, upturn and remove the tin. Place a second wire tray on the top, and upturn again.

6. Leave to cool on the tray then melt the white chocolate and drizzle in fine swirling lines. Separate the bars when the chocolate has set.

FINNISH GINGERS

INGREDIENTS
Makes 50

Metric		Imperial
85g	Margarine	3oz
60g	Caster sugar	2oz
115g	Lyle's golden syrup	4oz
200g	Self-raising flour	7oz
2.5ml	Ground cinnamon	½tsp
2.5ml	Ground ginger	½tsp
2.5ml	Ground cloves	½tsp
2.5ml	Bicarbonate of soda	½tsp
5ml	Water	1tsp

BAKING TRAYS

Lightly greased baking trays.

BAKING

Preheated oven, 150°C, 300°F
or gas mark 2
Middle shelf
10-15 minutes or until golden brown

Mary's Tips

Cut slices as thinly as possible
to make a crisper biscuit.
The thinner the biscuit the less
baking time required.

1. Melt the margarine, sugar and syrup over gentle heat. Sift the flour and spices then stir into the mixture.

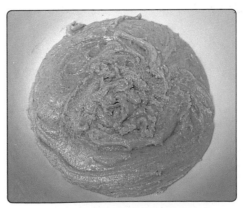

2. Dissolve the bicarbonate of soda in the water and mix in to form a soft dough. Cover the bowl and leave overnight in a cool place.

3. Mould the dough into a small loaf shape about 20.5cm (8in) long. Cut into thin slices, place onto trays and bake.

COCONUT MUNCHIES

1. Cream the vegetable fat, margarine and sugar until light and fluffy. Gradually beat in the egg a little at a time.

2. Fold in the flour and half the coconut. Add the lemon juice and mix until well blended.

INGREDIENTS
Makes 24

Metric		Imperial
85g	Vegetable fat	3oz
30g	Margarine	1oz
85g	Caster sugar	3oz
	1 egg, size 3, beaten	
145g	Self-raising flour	5oz
60g	Desiccated coconut	2oz
10ml	Lemon juice	2tbsp

DECORATION

Glacé cherries, halved

BAKING TRAYS

Well greased baking trays.

BAKING

Preheated oven, 190°C, 375°F or gas mark 5
Middle shelf
10-12 minutes or until golden brown

Mary's Tips

Because vegetable fats and lard have less liquid they contain the most shortening power.

3. Mould the mixture into walnut sized pieces, then roll in the remaining coconut, place on the trays well apart. Top each with half a glacé cherry and bake.

MARBLED BARS

1. Blend the cocoa and hot water together and leave to cool. Place the remaining ingredients into a mixing bowl and beat for 2-3 minutes on medium speed.

2. Divide the mixture into two equal portions. Stir the cocoa mixture into one portion until well blended.

INGREDIENTS
Makes 16

Metric		Imperial
15ml	Cocoa powder	1tbsp
15ml	Boiling water	1tbsp
170g	Soft tub margarine	6oz
170g	Caster sugar	6oz
170g	Self-raising flour	6oz
7.5ml	Baking powder	1½tsp
	3 eggs, size 3	

BAKING TIN

Greased and fully lined with greaseproof paper 18 x 28cm (7 x 11in) shallow baking tin.

BAKING

Preheated oven, 170°C, 340°F or gas mark 3
Middle shelf
Approximately 25 minutes or when firm to the touch

Mary's Tips

When cooked this traybake should spring back when lightly pressed on the top, and have slightly shrunk from the sides of the tin.

3. Using a dessert spoon, place alternate spoonfuls of mixture into the tin and then bake. Leave to cool in the tin for 10 minutes then turn out onto a wire tray to cool.

EMPIRE BISCUITS

INGREDIENTS
Makes 24

Metric		Imperial
85g	Margarine	3oz
60g	Lyle's golden syrup	2oz
	1 egg yolk	
145g	Plain flour	5oz
30g	Cornflour	1oz
10ml	Cinnamon	2tsp

FILLING

Jam or preserve of choice

TOPPING

See page 27 for water icing

BAKING TRAYS

Well greased baking trays.

BAKING

Preheated oven, 180°C, 360°F
or gas mark 4
Middle shelf
Approximately 10 minutes or just
brown around the edges

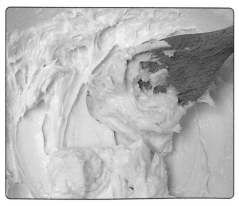

1. Thoroughly cream the margarine, syrup and egg yolk together.

2. Sift together the flour, cornflour and cinnamon then blend into the creamed mixture to form a smooth dough.

3. Roll out thinly on a lightly floured surface, cut out with a fluted cutter and bake. When cold, sandwich together with jam then coat the tops with feathered water icing.

INGREDIENTS
Makes 18

Metric		Imperial
285g	Light brown soft sugar	10oz
340g	Plain flour	12oz
170g	Butter, melted	6oz

FILLING

400g	Cream cheese	14oz
60g	Lyle's golden syrup	2oz
225g	Caster sugar	8oz
	2 eggs, size 3, beaten	
30ml	Lemon juice	2tbsp
60ml	Milk	4tbsp
5ml	Vanilla essence	1tsp

BAKING TIN

Well greased 18 x 28cm (7 x 11in) shallow baking tin.

BAKING

Preheated oven, 180°C, 360°F or gas mark 4
Middle shelf
20 minutes for the base, then 10 minutes with the filling and finally 20 minutes with the topping.

Mary's Tips

This cheese traybake also makes an ideal dessert, served hot or cold.

Can be served with strawberries or other fruits.

Be very careful when you remove from tin. It is best cooled completely in the tin first.

1. Combine the brown sugar and flour in a large bowl, stir in the melted butter until the mixture resembles breadcrumbs.

2. Fill the tin with two thirds of the mixture then press down evenly and firmly. Bake for 20 minutes.

3. Meanwhile beat the cream cheese, syrup and caster sugar until smooth.

4. Beat in the egg, lemon juice, milk and vanilla essence.

5. After the base has cooked, remove from the oven and leave for 2 minutes then pour on the creamed filling. Return to the oven for 10 minutes.

6. Then carefully remove and sprinkle on the remaining crumb mixture and bake for the last 20 minutes. Leave to cool in the tin, cut into fingers.

NUTTY WAFERS

1. Beat the margarine, sugar and syrup together until light and fluffy. Thoroughly beat in the egg and vanilla essence.

2. Sift the flour and bicarbonate of soda together, lightly stir into the mixture with the peanuts to form a soft dough.

3. Place walnut sized rounds onto the trays and bake. Leave on the tray for a few moments before cooling on wire trays.

INGREDIENTS

Makes 36

Metric		Imperial
115g	Margarine	4oz
60g	Caster sugar	2oz
170g	Lyle's golden syrup	6oz
	1 egg, size 3	
5ml	Vanilla essence	½tsp
145g	Plain flour	5oz
2.5ml	Bicarbonate of soda	¼tsp
85g	Roasted peanuts	3oz

BAKING TRAYS

Well greased trays or trays lined with parchment paper.

BAKING

Preheated oven, 180°C or 360°F or gas mark 4

Middle Shelf

Approximately 15 minutes or until golden brown.

Mary's Tips

Never warm syrup in a plastic bowl in a microwave as this may melt.

Good with ice cream.

153

VIENNESE SHELLS

1. Using a wooden spoon, beat the fat and icing sugar until creamy.

2. Gradually work in the flour to form a soft dough. Place a star savoy tube into a piping bag and fill with the mixture.

INGREDIENTS
Makes 30

Metric		Imperial
170g	Butter or margarine	6oz
60g	Icing sugar, sifted	2oz
170g	Plain flour, sifted	6oz

DECORATION

Glacé cherries, halved
Plain or milk Scotbloc or Chocolat, melted

BAKING TRAYS

Well greased baking trays.

BAKING

Preheated oven, 150°C, 300°F
or gas mark 2
Middle shelf
20-30 minutes or until lightly brown

Mary's Tips

Viennese can be piped as shells, rosettes, fingers and stars.

3. Pipe shells onto the trays. Place a half glacé cherry on some shells then bake. When cold dip some of the shells into melted chocolate (see page 15).

WHOLEWHEAT CRUNCHIES

1. Place the dry ingredients in a bowl, add butter cut into small pieces and rub in until breadcrumb consistency.

2. Add the egg and mix with a fork until the mixture holds together. Place onto a floured surface and knead until smooth. Cover and leave for 10 minutes.

3. Roll out to the required size. Place onto the tray and cut into sections then bake.

INGREDIENTS
Makes 8

Metric		Imperial
145g	Wholewheat flour	5oz
1.25ml	Salt	¼tsp
2.5ml	Baking powder	½tsp
30g	Caster sugar	1oz
85g	Butter	3oz
	1 egg, size 4	

BAKING TRAY

Baking tray lightly dusted with flour.

BAKING

Preheated oven, 180°C, 360°F
or gas mark 4
Middle shelf
10-15 minutes or until golden brown

155

GINGER TOPPED SHORTCAKE

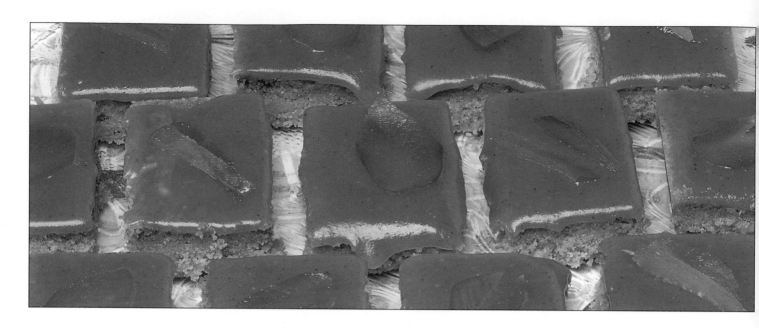

INGREDIENTS
Makes 16

Metric		Imperial
115g	Margarine	4oz
60g	Caster sugar	2oz
145g	Plain flour	5oz
10ml	Ground ginger	2tsp

TOPPING

60ml	Icing sugar, sifted	4tbsp
10ml	Ground ginger	2tsp
30g	Lyle's golden syrup	1oz
60g	Margarine	2oz

BAKING TIN

Well greased 20.5cm (8in) square shallow tin.

BAKING

Preheated oven, 170°C, 340°F or gas mark 3
Middle shelf
25-30 minutes or until golden brown

Mary's Tips

Do not boil the topping too much.

Pour the topping on quickly.

Decorate with pieces of preserved ginger for extra bite.

1. Cream the margarine and sugar together until light and fluffy. Sift the flour and ginger together then stir into the mixture. Knead together to form a smooth, firm dough.

2. Roll out and fit evenly into the base of the tin and bake. Leave to cool after baking. For the topping, place all the ingredients into a saucepan and bring to the boil.

3. Leave to cool slightly then spread evenly over the shortcake. Leave to set in a cold place before removing from the tin and cutting.

CINNAMON BISCUITS

INGREDIENTS
Makes 20

Metric		Imperial
170g	Plain flour, sifted	6oz
2.5ml	Ground cinnamon	½tsp
115g	Unsalted butter	4oz
60g	Caster sugar	2oz
	1 egg, size 4, beaten	

TOPPING

15ml	Granulated sugar	1tbsp
2.5ml	Ground cinnamon	½tsp
30g	Flaked almonds	1oz

BAKING TIN

Well greased 18 x 28cm (7 x 11in) shallow baking tin.

BAKING

Preheated oven, 170°C, 340°F or gas mark 3
Middle shelf
Approximately 15 minutes or until golden brown

1. Sift the flour and cinnamon together into a large bowl. Rub in the butter until the mixture resembles fine breadcrumbs, stir in the sugar.

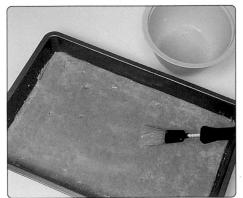

2. Place the mixture into the tin and press to form an even base. Brush with the beaten egg.

3. Mix the topping ingredients together then sprinkle onto the base and bake. Cut into shapes whilst still warm.

ICED and SPICED TREATS

1. Cut the butter into pieces and place in a large bowl. Place the sugar, treacle and spices into a saucepan and bring to boil. Add the bicarbonate of soda and pour into the bowl.

2. Stir until the butter has melted then beat in the egg. Stir in the flour. Knead the mixture to form a smooth manageable dough.

3. Roll out on lightly floured surface to 6mm (¼in) thickness. Cut into heart shapes, place onto trays and bake. Using recipe on page 27, decorate as required when cold.

INGREDIENTS
Makes 50

Metric		Imperial
115g	Butter	4oz
100g	Demerara sugar	3½oz
200g	Lyle's black treacle	7oz
5ml	Ground ginger	1tsp
5ml	Ground cinnamon	1tsp
2.5ml	Ground cloves	½tsp
5ml	Bicarbonate of soda	1tsp
	1 egg, size 3	
510g	Plain flour, sifted	1lb2oz

DECORATION

1 Egg white
Icing sugar (see page 27)
Various food colours
Nuts, finely chopped

BAKING TRAYS

Well greased baking trays.

BAKING

Preheated oven, 170°C, 340°F
or gas mark 3
Middle shelf
Approximately 10-15 minutes or until golden brown

Mary's Tips
Any shaped cutter can be used.
Use royal icing to add names for
a party.

APPLE SULTANA TRAYBAKE

INGREDIENTS
Makes 12

Metric		Imperial
255g	Self-raising flour	9oz
	Pinch of salt	
30ml	Cornflour	2tbsp
2.5ml	Ground cloves	½tsp
85g	Margarine	3oz
5ml	Grated lemon rind	1tsp
70g	Light brown soft sugar	2½oz
	1 egg yolk	
90ml	Milk	6tbsp

FILLING

570g	Cooking apples, peeled, cored and sliced	1¼lb
15ml	Lemon juice	1tbsp
30ml	Water	2tbsp
5ml	Grated lemon rind	1tsp
60g	Sultanas	2oz
30ml	Lyle's golden syrup	2tbsp

DECORATION

Icing sugar for dusting

BAKING TIN

Lightly greased 18 x 28cm (7 x 11in) shallow baking tin.

BAKING

Preheated oven, 220°C, 425°F or gas mark 7
Middle shelf
Bake for 10 minutes then reduce heat to 190°C, 375°F or gas mark 5 and bake for further 20 minutes or until golden brown and the pastry is cooked through.

1. Sift the flour, salt, cornflour and ground cloves into a bowl. Rub in the margarine until the mixture resembles fine breadcrumbs.

2. Stir in the lemon rind and sugar, then bind to a pliable dough with the egg yolk and milk.

3. Knead on a lightly floured surface until smooth, then wrap in polythene and chill whilst making the filling.

4. Place the sliced apples, lemon juice and water in a pan and cook gently until just tender. Remove from the heat, stir in the lemon rind, fruit and syrup then leave until cold.

5. Roll out two thirds of the dough and line the tin. Spread the filling evenly over the pastry. Roll out the remaining dough and cut into narrow strips.

6. Twist the strips as shown, using a little dab of water to fix, and then bake. After baking dust with icing sugar then leave to cool in the tin before cutting into slices.

CHEESE BISCUITS

INGREDIENTS
Makes 14

Metric		Imperial
100g	Matured Cheddar cheese	3½oz
60g	Ready salted potato crisps	2oz
70g	Plain flour	2½oz
5ml	Icing sugar	1tsp
4ml	Mustard powder	¾tsp
	Pinch of cayenne pepper	
70g	Butter	2½oz

BAKING TRAYS

Well greased baking trays.

BAKING

Preheated oven, 190°C, 375°F
or gas mark 5
Middle shelf
Approximately 15 minutes or until
golden brown

Mary's Tips

Use a strong flavoured cheese
for maximum flavour.

1. Grate the cheese into a bowl. Crush the crisps lightly and mix in. Sift together the flour, icing sugar, mustard powder and cayenne pepper and stir into the mixture.

2. Melt the butter and stir into the mixture until well blended.

3. Divide the mixture into 14 pieces and place onto the trays in small heaps and bake. Leave to cool on the trays for 3-4 minutes then cool on a wire tray.

APRICOT FRUIT FINGERS

INGREDIENTS
Makes 24

Metric		Imperial
170g	Plain wholemeal flour	6oz
115g	Plain flour, sifted	4oz
5ml	Ground cinnamon	1tsp
170g	Soft tub margarine	6oz
30ml	Lyle's golden syrup	2tbsp
170g	No-need to soak apricots, chopped	6oz
85g	Mixed nuts, chopped	3oz
60g	Glacé cherries, chopped	3oz
	1 egg, size 3, beaten	
115ml	Unsweetened orange juice	4floz

BAKING TIN

Well greased 18 x 28cm (7 x 11in) shallow baking tin.

BAKING

Preheated oven, 190°C, 375°F or gas mark 5
Middle shelf
Bake the base for 20 minutes, add the topping, then bake for a further 15 minutes or until topping is set but still soft.

1. Place 115g (4oz) of wholemeal flour with the plain flour and cinnamon into a bowl. Mix in the margarine and syrup.

2. Mix well to form a soft dough then roll out and fit evenly into the tin and bake for 20 minutes.

3. Meanwhile make the topping. Mix together the remaining wholemeal flour, chopped fruits and nuts until well blended. Then stir in the egg and orange juice.

4. Remove the biscuit base from the oven after 20 minutes then spread on the topping evenly and bake for another 15 minutes. Leave to cool in the tin then cut into bars.

MELTING MOMENTS

1. Cream the butter and sugar until light and fluffy. Then gradually beat in the egg.

2. Gently fold in the sifted flour. Roll the mixture on floured surface and divide into 16 pieces.

3. Mould each piece into a ball then roll in the oats to cover. Place onto the trays, flatten slightly then bake. After baking place half a cherry on each biscuit then leave until cold.

INGREDIENTS
Makes 16

Metric		Imperial
60g	Butter	2oz
60g	Caster sugar	2oz
	1 egg, size 3	
115g	Self-raising flour, sifted	4oz

DECORATION

Rolled oats
Coloured glacé cherries

BAKING TRAYS

Well greased baking trays.

BAKING

Preheated oven, 180°C or 360°F
or gas mark 4
Middle Shelf
15-20 minutes or until golden brown

Mary's Tips

Allow the eggs to stand out of the refrigerator overnight to reach room temperature before using.

Place well apart on the trays.

KATIES KRUNCH

1. Crush the biscuits into a bowl. Sift in the icing sugar and coconut. Mix well. Melt chocolate (see page 15). Stir in the butter and add to the crumbled biscuits.

2. Spread the mixture into the tin and chill for a few minutes. Melt the white chocolate over hot water then spread evenly over the top.

3. Immediately sprinkle with toasted coconut. Leave in the refrigerator for 1 hour. Turn out and cut into fingers.

INGREDIENTS
Makes 28

Metric		Imperial
115g	Wheatmeal biscuits	4oz
60g	Icing sugar	2oz
30g	Desiccated coconut	1oz
145g	Plain Scotbloc or Chocolat	5oz
115g	Butter	4oz

TOPPING

115g	White Scotbloc	4oz

DECORATION

A little toasted desiccated coconut

BAKING TIN

Lightly greased 20.5cm (8in) square shallow baking tin.

Mary's Tips

Remember to chill the mixture for just a few moments before adding the topping as the chocolate may separate when cut.

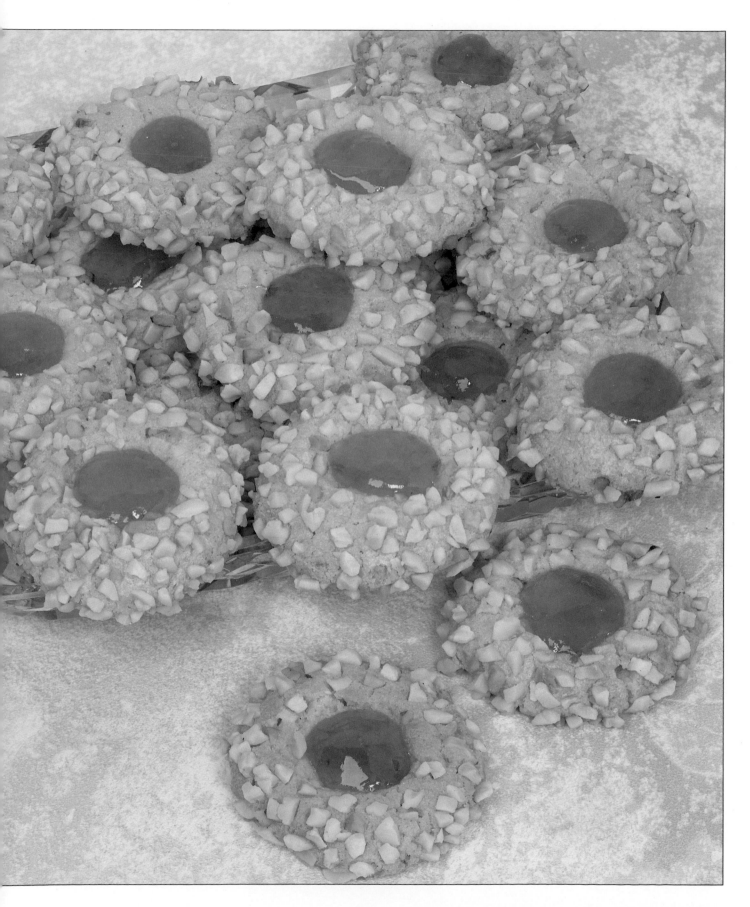

INGREDIENTS
Makes 24

Metric		Imperial
115g	Butter	4oz
60g	Caster sugar	2oz
30g	Lyle's golden syrup	1oz
	1 egg, size 3, separated	
145g	Plain flour, sifted	5oz

DECORATION

115g	Chopped nuts	4oz
	Apricot Pureé	

BAKING TRAYS

Well greased baking trays.

BAKING

Preheated oven, 170°C, 340°F
or gas mark 3
Middle shelf

15-20 minutes, pressing in the centres
again after the first 5 minutes of baking

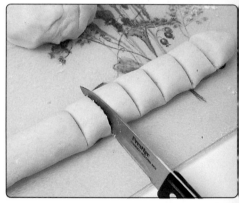

Mary's Tips

Apricot jam can be used for the centres if pushed through a sieve to achieve a smooth, clear texture.

Alternatively, seedless raspberry jam can be used.

Chopped almonds or peanuts can be used instead of chopped nuts.

1. Place the butter, sugar, syrup and egg yolk into a bowl and cream together.

2. Stir in the sifted flour to form a smooth dough. Chill in refrigerator until firm.

3. When chilled, divide the mixture in two, roll out and then cut each length into 12 pieces. Then roll into balls. Beat the egg white lightly in a small bowl.

4. Place the chopped nuts into another bowl. Dip three balls at a time into the egg white then roll in the nuts, using a fork.

5. Place onto greased trays then indent the tops with the handle of a wooden spoon.

6. Bake in the oven for five minutes then press the tops again. Continue baking until golden brown. When cold, pipe apricot pureé into the centres.

FLAPJACKS

INGREDIENTS

Makes 12

Metric		Imperial
170g	Rolled oats	6oz
115g	Light brown soft sugar	4oz
85g	Butter or margarine	3oz
60g	Lyle's golden syrup	2oz

DECORATION

A little plain or milk Scotbloc or Chocolat, melted

BAKING TIN

Well greased 28 x 18cm (11 x 7in) shallow baking tin.

BAKING

Preheated oven, 180°C, 360°F
or gas mark 4
Middle shelf
20minutes or until golden brown

Mary's Tips

It s very important to grease the tin well for this recipe.

Flapjacks can be dipped in melted chocolate.

1. Mix the oats and sugar together in a bowl, melt the butter and syrup together in a saucepan.

2. Mix the dry ingredients into the saucepan until well blended then spoon into the greased tin.

3. Press the mixture evenly into the tin then bake. After baking leave to cool slightly then cut into fingers or bars. Turn out when cold.

CHERRY PEEL BARS

1. Whisk the egg and sugar until foamy then beat in the syrup. Fold in the melted butter, essence, peel, almonds and cherries. Then carefully fold in the flour until well blended.

2. Pour the mixture into the greased tin and level out then bake in the preheated oven until golden brown.

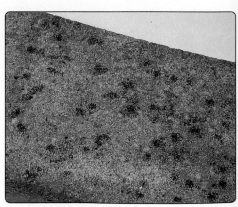

3. After baking, cool slightly then turn out onto greaseproof paper sprinkled with caster sugar. Sprinkle the top with more caster sugar. When cold cut into fingers as required.

INGREDIENTS
Makes 20

Metric		Imperial
	2 eggs, size 3	
115g	Light brown soft sugar	4oz
115g	Lyle's golden syrup	4oz
30ml	Butter, melted	2tbsp
2.5ml	Vanilla essence	½tsp
30g	Candied peel, chopped	1oz
30g	Blanched almonds, chopped	1oz
60g	Glacé cherries, quartered	2oz
115g	Self-raising flour, sifted	4oz

BAKING TIN

Well greased 18 x 28cm (7 x 11in) shallow baking tin.

BAKING

Preheated oven, 180°C, 360°F or gas mark 4
Middle shelf
Approximately 45 minutes

FINISHING

Greaseproof paper
Caster sugar

HAZELNUT CLUSTERS

1. Sift the flour into a bowl then mix in the oats, chopped hazelnuts and sugar.

2. Melt the margarine in a saucepan, beat the egg in a bowl then mix both into the dry ingredients together with the treacle. Mix until well blended.

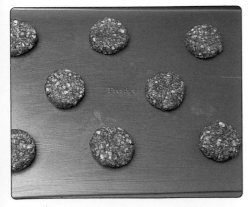

3. Form into small rounds about 1cm (½in) thick, place onto the trays and bake.

INGREDIENTS
Makes 30

Metric		Imperial
115g	Plain flour	4oz
225g	Rolled oats	8oz
115g	Hazelnuts, chopped	4oz
115g	Light brown soft sugar	4oz
115g	Margarine	4oz
	1 egg, size 3	
15ml	Lyle's black treacle	1tbsp

BAKING TRAYS

Lightly greased baking trays.

BAKING

Preheated oven, 200°C or 400°F or gas mark 5
Middle Shelf
15-20 minutes

Mary's Tips

Place a few sugar cubes with the biscuits in a tin to keep fresh and crisp.

GOLDEN OATIES

1. *Gently melt the butter with the syrup in a saucepan. Mix the flour, sugar, oats and ginger in a mixing bowl.*

2. *Stir in the melted butter together with the water until well blended.*

3. *Leave to cool for 5 minutes then mould into balls and place well apart on the trays and bake. After a few minutes transfer the biscuits onto a wire tray to cool.*

INGREDIENTS
Makes 30

Metric		Imperial
115g	Butter	4oz
30ml	Lyle's golden syrup	2tbsp
115g	Self-raising flour	4oz
115g	Light brown soft sugar	4oz
115g	Rolled oats	4oz
5ml	Ground ginger	1tsp
10ml	Water	2tsp

BAKING TRAYS

Well greased baking trays.

BAKING

Preheated oven, 150°C or 300°F or gas mark 2
Middle Shelf
Approximately 25 minutes

Mary's Tips

Measure golden syrup carefully. It will mix more readily with other ingredients if it slightly warmed.

ORANGE BARS

INGREDIENTS

Makes 16

Metric		Imperial
170g	Plain flour, sifted	6oz
60g	Semolina	2oz
85g	Caster sugar	3oz
170g	Butter or margarine	6oz
	Finely grated rind of 1 orange	

TOPPING

170g	Icing sugar, sifted	6oz
	Orange juice	

BAKING TIN

Well greased 18cm (7in) square, shallow baking tin.

BAKING

Preheated oven, 170°C, 340°F or gas mark 3
Middle shelf
Approximately 45 minutes or until firm to the touch, then add the topping and bake for a further 10 minutes

Mary's Tips

Do not overbake the topping.

Before grating, scrub the oranges to remove the wax coating. Use a coarse grater.

Lemon or lime can be used instead of orange for the biscuit and the topping.

1. Mix the flour, semolina and sugar together in a bowl. Rub the butter or margarine into the mixture to form breadcrumb texture. Mix in the grated orange rind.

2. Spoon the mixture into the tin and firm down evenly with a spatula and then bake. Meanwhile, mix the icing sugar and orange juice to make a thick coating consistency.

3. Spread over the biscuit when baked and return to the oven for 10 more minutes. Then leave in the tin to cool before cutting.

POLKA DOTS

1. Sift the flour into a mixing bowl then add the fat, sugar and eggs. Beat with a wooden spoon for 4 minutes, or with an electric beater for 2 minutes.

2. Fold in the coconut, milk and essence until well blended. Gently fold in the sugar coated chocolate drops.

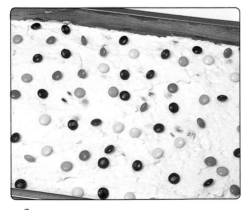

3. Spread the mixture evenly in the tin. Sprinkle chocolate drops on top and bake. After baking leave for 2-3 minutes before turning out onto a wire tray to cool. Cut into squares.

INGREDIENTS
Makes 16

Metric		Imperial
145g	Self-raising flour	5oz
115g	Margarine or butter, softened	4oz
115g	Caster sugar	4oz
	2 eggs, size 3	
60g	Dessicated coconut	2oz
2.5ml	Vanilla essence	½tsp
30ml	Milk	2tbsp
60g	Sugar coated chocolate drops	2oz

DECORATION

30g	Sugar coated chocolate drops	1oz

BAKING TIN

Greased and floured 18 x 28cm (7 x 11in) shallow baking tin.

BAKING

Preheated oven, 180°C, 360°F or gas mark 4
Middle shelf
25-30 minutes or until springy to the touch

Mary's Tips

Mix in the sugar coated chocolate drops as quickly as possible to avoid the coloured sugar dissolving in the mixture.

Chocolate drops can be used instead of sugar coated drops.

COCONUT BARS

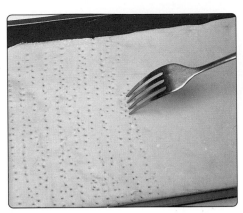

1. To make the base, sift the flour into a bowl, add the margarine and rub between fingers until mixture resembles breadcrumbs. Mix in the sugar.

2. Add about 30ml (2tbsp) of water and mix with a knife then knead to form a pastry. Roll out and fit into the tin, prick with a fork then bake for 20 minutes.

3. For the filling, whisk the eggs, brown sugar and essence together in a bowl until light and fluffy.

Mary's Tips

Use cream cheese, icing sugar and lemon juice as an alternative topping.

When toasting coconut, watch it closely to avoid burning.

4. Sift the flour, salt and baking powder together then fold into the mixture with the coconut to form a crumbly texture.

5. Spread onto the cooked base and lightly press evenly with a spatula. Bake in the oven for 10 minutes then leave in the tin until cold.

6. For the topping, toast the coconut until golden brown. Sift the icing sugar into a large bowl, melt the margarine and stir into the icing sugar with the lemon juice.

7. Spread over the top using a serrated scraper or fork to create a wavy pattern. Sprinkle with the toasted coconut then cut into squares.

INGREDIENTS
Makes 24

Metric		Imperial
145g	Plain flour	5oz
85g	Margarine	3oz
85g	Caster sugar	3oz
	Cold water to mix	

TOPPING

30g	Desiccated coconut	1oz
225g	Icing sugar	8oz
30g	Margarine	1oz
30ml	Lemon juice	2tbsp

FILLING

2 eggs, size 3

60g	Light brown soft sugar	2oz
5ml	Vanilla essence	1tsp
60g	Plain flour	2oz
1.25ml	Salt	¼tsp
7.5ml	Baking powder	1½tsp
285g	Desiccated coconut	10oz

BAKING TIN

Well greased 18 x 28cm (7 x 11in) shallow baking tin.

BAKING

Preheated oven, 180°C, 360°F or gas mark 4
Middle shelf
Bake the base for 20 minutes or until golden brown, add the filling then continue baking for 10 minutes.

COFFEE DROPS

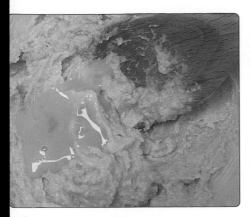

1. Cream the margarine, sugar and syrup together. Beat in the egg then the coffee essence.

2. Sift the flour and cinnamon together then gradually blend into the mixture to form a soft, smooth dough.

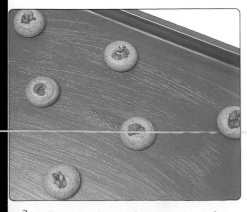

3. Fill a savoy bag and piping tube and then pipe small bulbs, well placed apart, onto the trays. Top with walnut pieces and bake.

INGREDIENTS
Makes 36

Metric		Imperial
60g	Margarine	2oz
60g	Light brown soft sugar	2oz
85g	Lyle's golden syrup	3oz
15ml	Egg, beaten	1tbsp
10ml	Coffee essence	2tsp
85g	Self-raising flour	3oz
2.5ml	Ground cinnamon	½tsp

DECORATION

Broken walnuts (optional)

BAKING TRAYS

Well greased baking trays.

BAKING

Preheated oven, 180°C, 360°F or gas mark 4
Middle Shelf
Approximately 15 minutes

Mary's Tips

Extra care is needed when baking these biscuits as they will brown very quickly, especially when using a fan oven.

VIIKUNAKAKKU

1. *Beat the butter and sugar together until light and fluffy. Whisk together the eggs and rind then gradually beat into the mixture, adding a little flour to stop mixture separating.*

2. *Sift the flour and baking powder together twice. Mix the fruit in 30ml (2tbsp) of the flour and fold into the creamed mixture then stir in the remaining flour.*

3. *Spread evenly into the tin and bake. After baking leave in the tin for 10 minutes then out onto a wire tray to cool. When cold, dust with icing sugar and cut into bars.*

INGREDIENTS
Makes 24

Metric		Imperial
170g	Butter	6oz
115g	Light brown soft sugar	4oz
	3 eggs, size 2	
30ml	Orange rind, grated	2tbsp
170g	Plain flour	6oz
5ml	Baking powder	1tsp
70g	Dried figs, chopped	2½oz
70g	Seedless raisins	2½oz
30g	Walnuts, chopped	1oz

DECORATION

Icing sugar for dusting

BAKING TIN

Well grease then dust with caster sugar a 18 x 28cm (7 x 11in) shallow baking tin.

BAKING

Preheated oven, 180°C, 360°F or gas mark 4
Middle Shelf
40-45 minutes

Mary's Tips

This traybake is traditionally made in a ring mould.

Always use a very well greased tin.

GINGERBREAD SNAPS

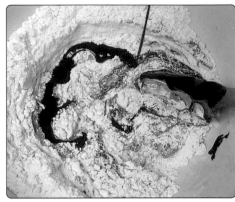

1. Put the treacle, butter and sugar into a small saucepan. Stir over low heat until the butter has melted. Sift the remaining ingredients together into a bowl.

2. When the treacle has cooled mix into the dry ingredients to form a soft, smooth dough. Turn out and divide in half. Roll to 25.5cm (10in) long and cut each into 10 pieces.

INGREDIENTS
Makes 20

Metric		Imperial
90ml	Lyle's black treacle	6tbsp
85g	Butter	3oz
60g	Light brown soft sugar	2oz
225g	Plain flour	8oz
2.5ml	Ground ginger	½tsp
2.5ml	Ground coriander	½tsp
1.25ml	Bicarbonate of soda	¼tsp

TOPPINGS

Desiccated coconut
Demerara sugar
Oatmeal
Flaked almonds
Ginger pieces

BAKING TRAYS

Well greased baking trays.

BAKING

Preheated oven, 180°C,
or gas mark 4
Just above middle shelf
8-10 minutes

Mary's Tips

When measuring the treacle ensure it is level in the spoon with the bottom of the spoon scraped clean.

In step 1, make sure the heat is low as the mixture should melt not cook.

3. Roll into balls and then into any of the suggested toppings, place onto trays and bake.

FLORENTINES

INGREDIENTS
Makes 20

Metric		Imperial
85g	Plain flour, sifted	3oz
60g	Sultanas	2oz
115g	Glacé cherries, chopped	4oz
170g	Flaked almonds	6oz
170g	Lyle's golden syrup	6oz
170g	Butter	6oz

DECORATION

225g	Plain or milk Scotbloc or Chocolat	8oz

BAKING TRAYS

Baking trays of appropriate sizes with paper cases.

BAKING

Preheated oven, 190°C, 375°F
or gas mark 5
Middle shelf
10-12 minutes

Mary's Tips

If paper cases are not used, watch the edges do not burn.

1. Mix together the flour, sultanas, glacé cherries and flaked almonds in a bowl. Place the syrup and butter into a saucepan and melt.

2. As soon as the butter has melted remove from the heat and stir in the mixed ingredients until well blended.

3. Spread small amounts into the baking cases or directly onto trays (see Mary's Tips) and bake. Leave to cool on the trays then coat the undersides with melted chocolate.

ALMOND and MINCEMEAT FINGERS

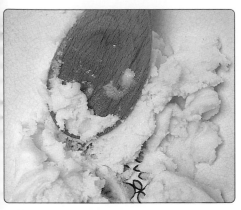

INGREDIENTS
Makes 14

Metric		Imperial
85g	Butter or margarine	3oz
85g	Caster sugar	3oz
	1 egg, size 3	
	2 drops almond essence	
170g	Plain flour	6oz
85g	Ground almonds	3oz

FILLING

225g	Mincemeat	8oz
	Grated rind of 1	
	small lemon.	

TOPPING

30g	Flaked almonds	1oz

1. Place fat and sugar into a bowl. Separate the egg then add the yolk. Add essence then mix to form a smooth paste. Work in most of the egg white – reserving 1 teaspoon.

2. Mix together the flour and ground almonds then add to the mixture. Mix until a smooth pastry is formed.

BAKING TIN

Well greased 18 x 28cm (7 x 11in) shallow baking tin.

BAKING

Preheated oven, 180°C, 360°F or gas mark 4
Middle shelf
Approximately 20 minutes

3. Divide the pastry in half, roll out and press into the base of the tin.

4. Spread the mincemeat on top then the grated lemon rind.

Mary's Tips

For variations of the filling add a little cooked apple to the mincemeat. Or use 450g (1lb) cooked apples with 60g (2oz) of sultanas instead of the mincemeat.

5. Roll out the remaining pastry and lightly press onto the top. Brush with the remaining egg white and sprinkle on the flaked almonds.

6. Leave in a cool place for 30 minutes. Mark into 14 fingers then bake. After baking gently lift out the fingers onto a wire tray to cool.

MONKEY PUZZLES

1. Sift together the flour and cocoa powder, twice. Cream the margarine and syrup until soft.

2. Stir in the flour. Coarsely crush the cornflakes and stir into the mixture until well blended.

3. Place spoonfuls, walnut size, onto greased trays and bake. When cold, dip tops into melted chocolate (see page 15) and decorate as required.

INGREDIENTS
Makes 20

Metric		Imperial
70g	Plain flour	2½oz
22.5ml	Cocoa powder	1½tbsp
85g	Margarine	3oz
85g	Lyle's golden syrup	3oz
30g	Crisp cornflakes	1oz

DECORATION

Plain or milk Scotbloc or Chocolat, melted

White Scotbloc, melted

BAKING TRAYS

Well greased baking trays.

BAKING

Preheated oven, 180°C, 360°F or gas mark 4
Middle Shelf
Approximately 12 minutes

Mary's Tips

To drizzle chocolate, fill a small piping bag and cut a tiny hole at the tip. Squeeze gently and move backwards and forwards.

CRISPY OVALS

INGREDIENTS
Makes 24

Metric		Imperial
	2 rashers back bacon	
115g	Plain wholemeal flour	4oz
1.25ml	Ground coriander	¼tsp
	Good pinch of	
	cayenne pepper	
85g	Butter	3oz
85g	Matured Cheddar	3oz
	cheese, grated	
15-20ml	Milk	3-4tsp
15ml	Lyle's golden syrup	1tbsp
	Milk for glazing	

Sesame seeds
Poppy seeds
Parmesan cheese, grated

BAKING TRAYS

Well greased baking trays.

BAKING

Preheated oven, 190°C, 375°F
or gas mark 5
Middle Shelf
10 minutes or until lightly browned

Mary's Tips

Other savoury toppings could be used such as anchovies or roasted chopped peppers.

For cocktail biscuits, use a small cutter.

These biscuits make an excellent base for hors d'oevres.

1. Derind the bacon, cut into pieces and fry until very crisp. Drain on kitchen paper. Sift the flour, coriander and pepper together then mix in the butter forming a crumb texture.

2. Chop the bacon finely then add to the mixture with the cheese. Mix together to form a pliable dough, adding sufficient milk as required.

3. Roll the dough on surface dusted with wholemeal flour. Cut into fluted ovals and place onto the trays. Brush with milk, sprinkle on various toppings and bake.

CHRISTMAS COOKIES

1. Place the margarine or butter, sugar, sifted flour, milk and syrup into a bowl. Mix the ingredients together, using a wooden spoon or electric beater, until it forms a soft dough.

2. Turn out onto lightly floured surface and knead. Gently roll out the dough and cut shapes as required.

INGREDIENTS

Metric		Imperial
115g	Soft tub margarine or Butter	4oz
145g	Caster sugar	5oz
225g	Plain flour, sifted	8oz
45ml	Milk	3tbsp
15ml	Lyle's golden syrup	1tbsp

DECORATION

A little royal icing
Plain or milk Scotbloc or Chocolat, melted

BAKING TRAYS

Well greased baking trays.

BAKING

Preheated oven, 190°C, 375°F or gas mark 5
Middle shelf
15 minutes or until pale golden in colour

Mary's Tips

Do not overknead the dough as otherwise a tough biscuit will result.

Wrap the cookies in coloured foil and hang on the Christmas tree.

3. Place onto the greased trays and bake. After baking leave for 5 minutes then cool on wire trays. Decorate with chocolate for feet and royal icing for the snow.

SANTA'S BISCUITS

INGREDIENTS
Makes 30

Metric		Imperial
115g	Butter	4oz
115g	Caster sugar	4oz
	1 egg, size 2, lightly beaten	
225g	Plain flour	8oz
	Pinch of salt	
	Grated rind of 1 small orange	

DECORATION

A little sugarpaste and royal icing

BAKING TRAYS

Well greased baking trays.

BAKING

Preheated oven, 180°C, 360°F
or gas mark 4
Middle shelf
15 minutes or until pale golden in
colour

Mary's Tips

Sugarpaste can be purchased
from most supermarkets.

1. Cream the butter and sugar until light, white and fluffy. Thoroughly beat in the egg, a little at a time.

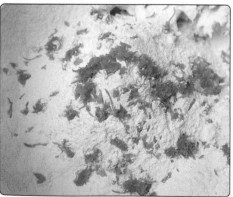

2. Sift the flour and salt together twice, then gently fold into the mixture with the grated orange rind. Mix to a firm dough.

3. Wrap in greaseproof paper and chill for 30 minutes. Roll out, not too thin, cut shapes required and bake. When baked, leave on a wire tray to cool then decorate as required.

ACKNOWLEDGEMENTS

Many thanks to:

TATE AND LYLE SUGARS - Carmel Keens is the Senior Home Economist and is a highly respected and knowledgeable figure in cookery circles. Her expertise is wide ranging, covering everything from cake decoration, recipe testing, new product development, to budget meals and health education in schools. She is sugar adviser to cookery editors, having produced many of the Tate and Lyle Sugars recipe leaflets and booklets. She is involved in travelling the country to attend trade shows and many major food exhibitions.

PRESTIGE GROUP UK PLC for supplying cake tins, cookware and decorating items used in this book.

R & W SCOTT LIMITED for providing all the chocolate used in this book.

ISBN: 0 9462429 58 8

MARY FORD TITLES

101 Cake Designs
ISBN: 0 946429 00 6   320 pages
The original Mary Ford cake artistry text book. A classic in its field, over 200,000 copies sold.

Cake Making and Decorating
ISBN: 0 946429 41 3   96 pages
Mary Ford divulges all the skills and techniques cake decorators need to make and decorate a variety of cakes in every medium.

Jams, Chutneys and Pickles
ISBN: 0 946429 48 0   96 pages
Over 70 of Mary Ford's favourite recipes for delicious jams, jellies, pickles and chutneys with hints and tips for perfect results.

Kid's Cakes
ISBN: 0 946429 53 7   96 pages
33 exciting new Mary Ford designs and templates for children's cakes in a wide range of mediums.

Children's Birthday Cakes
ISBN: 0 946429 46 4   112 pages
The book to have next to you in the kitchen! Over forty new cake ideas for children's cakes with an introduction on cake making and baking to ensure the cake is both delicious as well as admired.

Party Cakes
ISBN: 0 946429 13 8   120 pages
36 superb party time sponge cake designs and templates for tots to teenagers. An invaluable prop for the party cake decorator.

Quick and Easy Cakes
ISBN: 0 946429 42 1   208 pages
The book for the busy mum. 99 new ideas for party and special occasion cakes.

Decorative Sugar Flowers for Cakes
ISBN: 0 946429 51 0   120 pages
33 of the highest quality handcrafted sugar flowers with cutter shapes, background information and appropriate uses.

Cake Recipes
ISBN: 0 946429 43 X   96 pages
Contains 60 of Mary's favourite cake recipes ranging from fruit cake to cinnamon crumble cake.

One Hundred Easy Cake Designs
ISBN: 0 946429 47 2   208 pages
Mary Ford has originated 100 cakes all of which have been selected for ease and speed of making. The ideal book for the busy parent or friend looking for inspiration for a special occasion cake.

Wedding Cakes
ISBN: 0 946429 39 1   96 pages
For most cake decorators, the wedding cake is the most complicated item they will produce. This book gives a full step-by-step description of the techniques required and includes over 20 new cake designs.

Home Baking with Chocolate
ISBN: 0 946429 54 5   96 pages
Over 60 tried and tested recipes for cakes, gateaux, biscuits, confectionery and desserts. The ideal book for busy mothers.

Making Cakes for Money
ISBN: 0 946429 44 8   120 pages
The complete guide to making and costing cakes for sale at stalls or to friends. Invaluable advice on costing ingredients and time accurately.

Biscuit Recipes
ISBN: 0 946429 50 2   96 pages
Nearly 100 biscuit and traybake recipes chosen for their variety and ease of making. Full introduction for beginners.

The New Book of Cake Decorating
ISBN: 0 946429 59 6   224 pages
The most comprehensive title in the Mary Ford list. It includes over 100 new cake designs and full descriptions of all the latest techniques.

A to Z of Cake Decorating
ISBN: 0 946429 52 9   208 pages
New dictionary style home cake decorating book with step-by-step examples covering techniques and skills of the craft. Suitable for the beginner and enthusiast alike.

Novelty Cakes
                                        120 pages
ISBN: 0 946429 56 1
Over 40 creative ideas to make a successful party. Introduction and basic recipes for beginners with a full step-by-step guide to each cake design.

BOOKS BY MAIL ORDER

Mary Ford operates a mail order service for all her step-by-step titles. If you write to Mary at the address below she will provide you with a price list and details. In addition, all names on the list receive information on new books and special offers. Mary is delighted, if required, to write a personal message in any book purchased by mail order.

Write to: Mary Ford,
            30 Duncliff Road,
            Southbourne, Bournemouth,
            Dorset. BH6 4LJ. U.K.

INDEX

INDEX
Continued